CONTENTS

The period of Earth's history between 245 and 65 million years ago is often known as the Age of **Dinosaurs**. There were thousands of different dinosaurs; most were peaceful **herbivores**, but some were ferocious, meat-eating predators. This section presents our Top Ten of the most dangerous dinosaurs, rated according to:

BODY MASS

Size was obviously important for a dinosaur **predator**. The bigger the predator, the bigger the **prey** it can attack. Similarly with weight, a heavy predator will find it easier to drag down and overpower its prey. We gave our dinosaurs a combined score based on their size and weight, but also taking into consideration the average size of their prey in each case.

NO.9 — VELOCIRAPTOR

Velociraptor lived in Asia towards the end of the Cretaceous period. The first remains of this dinosaur were discovered in Mongolia by Henry Osborn in 1924. Velociraptor had a winning combination of speed, aggression and fearsome weapons – only its small size prevents it from being the overall winner. It was the size of a small turkey!

BODY MASS
An average Velociraptor would have been about 1.5 metres long, and just a metre tall at the hip. This dinosaur would have weighed about 20-25 kilograms.

JAW POWER
It had about 80 teeth that were designed for ripping and tearing flesh. Narrow jaws allowed Velociraptor to push its head inside the carcass of a dinosaur.

MOBILITY
Velociraptor was a fast-running bipedal dinosaur, capable of reaching speeds of 64 kph. Its name means "speedy thief."

8

JAW POWER

2/10

Most dinosaur predators relied entirely on their jaws for killing, as well as eating. We based our score on the size and strength of the **jaws**, together with the number, length, and sharpness of the teeth. Only a few dinosaurs, such as our overall winner Deinonychus, had claws that were also efficient weapons, and they were awarded bonus points.

MOBILITY

10/10

High speed gives a predator a tremendous advantage – but speed alone is not everything. There is no point in being able to run faster than your prey, if you cannot change direction easily, or come to a sudden stop. Our dinosaur predators were given points for their speed, acceleration, and agility; with extra points awarded to those with good jumping skills.

FRIGHT FACTOR

1/10

Meat-eating dinosaurs employed a wide variety of hunting techniques. Some were pack-hunters, while other lived and hunted alone. Some dinosaurs preferred to wait in ambush for their prey, while others were constantly on the prowl for something to eat. We based our scores on the overall efficiency of the technique that was most frequently employed.

HUNTING SKILLS

8/10

Some of the meat-eating dinosaurs were as big as a bus – and any predator that size is frightening. Exactly how frightening depends on how close you are. The closer you are, the less time you have to decide before you are eaten. The largest dinosaurs were not always the most frightening, however.

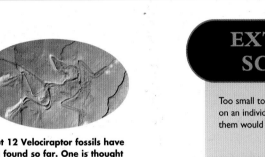

About 12 Velociraptor fossils have been found so far. One is thought to have died whilst fighting a Protoceratops.

Velociraptor (above right) was one of the fastest and fiercest predators that ever lived.

FRIGHT FACTOR

Velociraptor was not much larger than a pet cat, but you would not want to meet a pack of these vicious little dinosaurs.

HUNTING SKILLS

Velociraptor was a pack hunter and a highly efficient predator. It attacked with the claws of all four limbs, and could even jump up onto the back of its prey.

EXTREME SCORES

Too small to be more highly rated on an individual basis, but a pack of them would be a different matter.

MOBILITY **10/10**

BODY MASS **1/10**

JAW POWER **2/10**

FRIGHT FACTOR **1/10**

HUNTING SKILLS **8/10**

= TOTAL SCORE

Dilophosaurus lived during the early part of the **Jurassic** period. This **carnivore** had a distinctive **crest** made from a double layer of bone along the top of its skull. This colourful strip would have been used for communication. The **fossil** remains of Dilophosaurus were discovered in 1942 in Arizona, USA, by the **palaeontologist** Samuel Welles.

Dilophosaurus had an unusually long tail for an active predator.

BODY MASS

Dilophosaurus was about six metres in length, and weighed about 500 kilograms. It had a slender build but was a ferocious fighter.

MOBILITY

Dilophosaurus was a **bipedal** animal that hunted by chasing its prey. Powerful muscles in the hind limbs enabled it to run quickly.

JAW POWER

Although Dilophosaurus' **jaws** were packed with long sharp teeth, they were fairly weak.

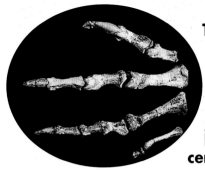

The claws at the ends of the fingers and toes were very sharp, but they were just a few centimetres long.

FRIGHT FACTOR

Dilophosaurus was big enough to look scary, but those jaws were not as strong as they looked. Its claws were deadly.

HUNTING SKILLS

Most scientists believe that Dilophosaurus hunted in packs, so it could attack animals much larger than itself. Some scientists, however, think that Dilophosaurus fed only on **carrion**.

This dinosaur just manages to get into our top ten because of its high score for mobility.

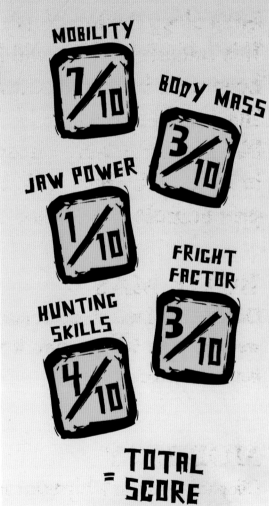

MOBILITY
7/10

BODY MASS
3/10

JAW POWER
1/10

FRIGHT FACTOR
3/10

HUNTING SKILLS
4/10

= TOTAL SCORE

VELOCIRAPTOR

Velociraptor lived in Asia towards the end of the **Cretaceous** period. The first remains of this dinosaur were discovered in Mongolia by Henry Osborn in 1924. Velociraptor had a winning combination of speed, aggression and fearsome weapons – only its small size prevents it from being the overall winner. It was the size of a small turkey!

BODY MASS

An average Velociraptor would have been about 1.5 metres long, and just a metre tall at the hip. This dinosaur would have weighed about 20-25 kilograms.

JAW POWER

It had about 80 teeth that were designed for ripping and tearing flesh. Narrow jaws allowed Velociraptor to push its head inside the **carcass** of a dinosaur.

MOBILITY

Velociraptor was a fast-running bipedal dinosaur, capable of reaching speeds of 64 kph. Its name means "speedy thief."

About 12 Velociraptor fossils have been found so far. One is thought to have died whilst fighting a Protoceratops.

Velociraptor (left) was one of the fastest and fiercest predators that ever lived.

FRIGHT FACTOR

Velociraptor was not much larger than a pet cat, but you would not want to meet a pack of these vicious little dinosaurs.

HUNTING SKILLS

Velociraptor was a pack hunter and a highly efficient predator. It attacked with the claws of all four limbs, and could even jump up onto the back of its prey.

Too small to be more highly rated on an individual basis, but a pack of them would be a different matter.

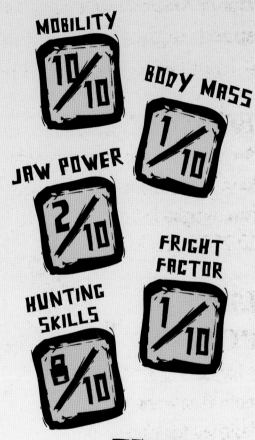

MOBILITY
10/10

BODY MASS
1/10

JAW POWER
2/10

FRIGHT FACTOR
1/10

HUNTING SKILLS
8/10

= TOTAL SCORE

GIGANOTOSAURUS

Palaeontologists believe that Giganotosaurus is the largest carnivore that ever walked the Earth. It is also one of the most mysterious of the meat-eating dinosaurs because it was not discovered until 1994. An amateur fossil-hunter named Ruben Carolini, made the discovery in Argentina in South America.

BODY MASS

Giganotosaurus is the largest flesh-eating dinosaur so far discovered. It was 16 metres long and weighed about 8,000 kilograms.

JAW POWER

The jaws were crammed with narrow, pointed teeth that had **serrated** edges for slicing through flesh. The biggest teeth were about 20 centimetres long.

MOBILITY

For such a large animal, Giganotosaurus could run surprisingly quickly at up to 24 kph. Its slim, pointed tail may have provided balance and quick turning whilst running.

A huge – 1.8-metre long – skull housed a very small brain.

FRIGHT FACTOR

Giganotosaurus was huge – bigger than Tyrannosaurus Rex – and looked very scary, but fortunately it seems to have been quite a rare dinosaur.

HUNTING SKILLS

Giganotosaurus hunted by charging at its prey with its jaws wide open. It attacked plant-eating dinosaurs that were more than 20 metres in length.

Giganotosaurus (shown here left and right) were capable of attacking and killing even large dinosaurs.

Too slow and too clumsy to be a serious contender.

MOBILITY
1/10

BODY MASS
10/10

JAW POWER
5/10

FRIGHT FACTOR
6/10

HUNTING SKILLS
1/10

= TOTAL SCORE

Troodon was a small bipedal dinosaur that lived at the very end of the Cretaceous period. In terms of brain-size to body weight, it may have been the brainiest animal on Earth at that time. The first Troodon fossil was discovered by Ferdinand V. Hayden in 1855. The US palaeontologist Joseph Leidy named the **species** in 1856.

In terms of overall body-shape, Troodon was very similar to a present-day **ostrich**.

BODY MASS

Troodon was about 2-3 metres long and weighed 40-50 kilograms. It would probably have been covered in feathers.

JAW POWER

This dinosaur had up to 100 curved teeth packed into its mouth. Each tooth had a wide, serrated edge for slicing through flesh.

MOBILITY

Long legs and light body weight allowed Troodon to take very big strides, so it could run extremely quickly – possibly faster than any other dinosaur.

These curving teeth are responsible for the name Troodon, which means "wounding tooth".

FRIGHT FACTOR

It was too small to be very scary during the day, but it would be a different matter if Troodon took you by surprise in dim light.

HUNTING SKILLS

Large, forward-facing eyes suggest to scientists that Troodon may have hunted small **mammals** in low-light conditions, either at night or at dawn and dusk.

Very fast, but a lightweight dinosaur that was only really scary at night.

MOBILITY
9/10

BODY MASS
2/10

JAW POWER
3/10

FRIGHT FACTOR
2/10

HUNTING SKILLS
9/10

= TOTAL SCORE

25/50

During the middle part of the Cretaceous period, this dinosaur was the top predator in North Africa. It had razor-sharp teeth, and it was big enough to attack and kill the largest plant-eating dinosaurs. German palaeontologists discovered Carcharodontosaurus in Morocco in 1925. Unfortunately, fossils of the dinosaur were destroyed during World War II.

BODY MASS

Carcharodontosaurus grew up to 15 metres in length – nearly as big as Giganotosaurus – and weighed more than 7,000 kilograms.

JAW POWER

This dinosaur had wide, powerful jaws the size of a human, with sharp teeth that could easily penetrate the toughest skin.

MOBILITY

Carcharodontosaurus was bipedal, but it relied on power and weight rather than speed and it could not run very quickly.

FRIGHT FACTOR

This dinosaur was big and very fierce, but it was also quite slow moving, so you could probably manage to run away if it spotted you.

A fragment of the dinosaur's skull and upper jaw.

The appearance of Carcharodontosaurus has been reconstructed from just a few fossil bones.

Low scores for speed and hunting are responsible for this giant killer not being more highly rated.

MOBILITY
2/10

BODY MASS
9/10

JAW POWER
4/10

FRIGHT FACTOR
9/10

HUNTING SKILLS
2/10

 TOTAL SCORE

26/50

HUNTING SKILLS

Carcharodontosaurus was probably an ambush hunter that waited in hiding until it could launch a surprise attack.

Albertosaurus was a sleek, saw-toothed predator that hunted **Hadrosaurs** and other plant-eating dinosaurs. It lived in North America during the last part of the Cretaceous period. Geologist Joseph Tyrell discovered fossils of Albertosaurus in 1884 in Alberta, Canada.

BODY MASS

Albertosaurus measured more than 8 metres in length, stood 4 metres high at the hip and weighed about 3,000 kilograms.

JAW POWER

Albertosaurus had a big head, with large, powerful jaws. There were about 36 razor-sharp teeth in its upper jaw, and about 30 in the lower jaw.

MOBILITY

This large bipedal dinosaur may have reached 31 kph when running at top speed, as fast as any other dinosaur of its size.

FRIGHT FACTOR

This was a very scary dinosaur because it combined large size with fast speed, which made it a deadly hunter.

This skull still has most of the teeth intact.

HUNTING SKILLS

Albertosaurus may not have been a very good hunter, because its eyes are positioned at the side of its head. Predators see better when their eyes are at the front.

Like other bipedal dinosaurs, Albertosaurus used its tail for balance.

This was a big, fast predator, but there were other dinosaurs that were bigger and faster.

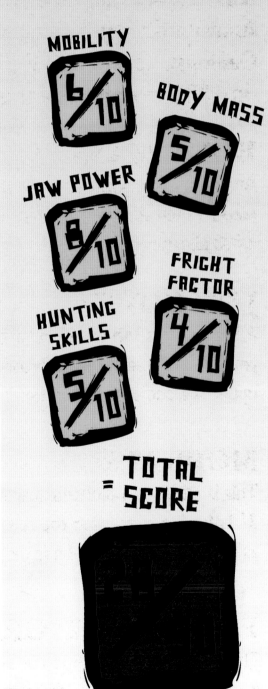

MOBILITY
6/10

BODY MASS
5/10

JAW POWER
8/10

FRIGHT FACTOR
4/10

HUNTING SKILLS
5/10

= TOTAL SCORE

Allosaurus was once the largest predator on Earth. It lived at the end of the Jurassic period and the beginning of the Cretaceous period. The first fossils were discovered in 1879 in Wyoming, USA, by the famous fossil-hunter Othniel C. Marsh.

BODY MASS

Allosaurus was about 12 metres long when fully grown. This giant also weighed more than 4,000 kilograms.

JAW POWER

Allosaurus had about 70 sharp teeth, and each tooth was up to 10 centimetres long. But the teeth were fragile, and broke off easily.

Allosaurus was capable of killing even the biggest plant-eating dinosaurs.

Allosaurus was a top predator with no natural enemies.

MOBILITY
This bipedal carnivore may have had a top speed of about 19 kph, but it had no **stamina** for a long chase.

FRIGHT FACTOR
This dinosaur was even bigger and more aggressive than Albertosaurus – just hope that it gets tired before you do!

HUNTING SKILLS
Allosaurus may have hunted in packs, using the 15-centimetre claws on its forelimbs to slash open its prey.

A serious contender for the number one spot – but its slow speed and lack of stamina reduce its overall scariness.

MOBILITY
4/10

BODY MASS
6/10

JAW POWER
9/10

FRIGHT FACTOR
5/10

HUNTING SKILLS
7/10

= TOTAL SCORE

SPINOSAURUS

Spinosaurus was a fierce predator that lived in Africa during the mid Cretaceous period. It had a strange 2-metre tall crest along its back that was made of long **spines** covered by tough skin. The first fossil of Spinosaurus was discovered in Egypt in 1912 by German palaeontologist Ernst Stromer von Reichenbach.

Spinosaurus looked as strange as any fairy tale dragon, but it was a real animal.

BODY MASS

Spinosaurus reached lengths of up to 15 metres, and weighed up to 7,000 kilograms.

JAW POWER

This dinosaur had long, narrow jaws lined with razor sharp, pointed teeth.

MOBILITY

The longer than usual forelimbs suggest that Spinosaurus may have walked on all fours at least some of the time.

Each tooth was designed to penetrate deeply into a prey's flesh.

HUNTING SKILLS

The design of the jaws and teeth suggest that Spinosaurus probably fed mainly on fish that it snatched from rivers and lakes.

FRIGHT FACTOR

This dinosaur is straight out of your worst nightmares – a gigantic heavyweight killer with jaws like a crocodile.

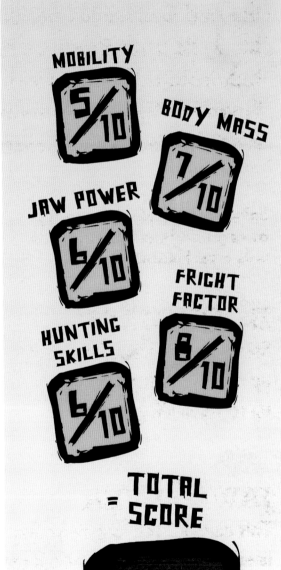

Spinosaurus was large and fierce – for a fish-eater – but a bit too slow to score any higher.

MOBILITY 5/10

BODY MASS 7/10

JAW POWER 6/10

FRIGHT FACTOR 8/10

HUNTING SKILLS 6/10

= TOTAL SCORE

TYRANNOSAURUS REX

This is the most famous of all the dinosaurs and one of the biggest land predators that has ever lived. It is often known as Tyrannosaurus Rex (or T Rex), because "rex" means "king" in the **Latin** language. The first fossils were discovered in 1908 in Montana, USA, by fossil-hunter Barnum Brown.

BODY MASS

Tyrannosaurus was 12 metres long and weighed more than 7,000 kilograms, but it had very puny little forelimbs that only grew to about 1 metre.

MOBILITY

This bipedal carnivore could run at speeds of up to 29 kph, but only over short distances.

JAW POWER

Tyrannosaurus had massive jaws with very powerful muscles, and it could bite straight through even the biggest bones.

This killer could tear off 200 kilograms of flesh with a single bite.

Tyrannosaurus was part of a family of dinosaurs called Tyrannosaurids. Above are three more types.

FRIGHT FACTOR

The sight of this monster charging at you would probably frighten you to death.

HUNTING SKILLS

Tyrannosaurus probably stalked herds of plant-eating dinosaurs and picked off the weakest members – the very young and the very old.

This massive and terrifying killer had huge jaws and hind limbs, but its forelimbs were definitely undersized.

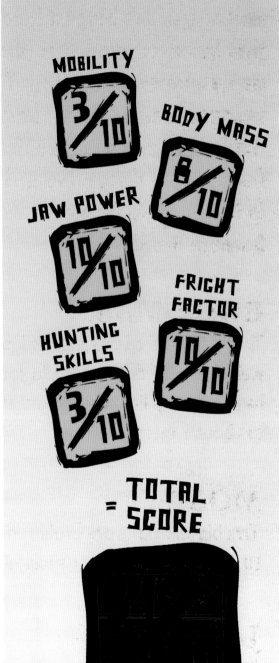

MOBILITY
3/10

BODY MASS
8/10

JAW POWER
10/10

FRIGHT FACTOR
10/10

HUNTING SKILLS
3/10

= TOTAL SCORE

DEINONYCHUS

Deinonychus was the supreme dinosaur predator – a fast and deadly pack hunter. It lived in North America during the early part of the Cretaceous period. Deinonychus was discovered in 1931 in Montana, USA, by fossil hunter Barnum Brown, and was named in 1964 by US palaeontologist John Ostrom.

BODY MASS

Deinonychus was a medium-sized carnivore that weighed about 80 kilograms and stood 2 metres tall.

JAW POWER

A combination of powerful **jaw** muscles and curved teeth with serrated edges meant that Deinonychus could bite off huge chunks of flesh.

MOBILITY

Deinonychus was a fast-running, **agile** predator that could attack with the claws of all four limbs as well as its teeth.

Each tooth could cut through skin and muscle like the blade of a knife.

The fastest, fiercest, and most fearsome – this dinosaur is enough to give even a Tyrannosaurus bad dreams.

MOBILITY
8/10

BODY MASS
4/10

JAW POWER
7/10

FRIGHT FACTOR
7/10

HUNTING SKILLS
10/10

= TOTAL SCORE

FRIGHT FACTOR

Just one of these dinosaurs was scary, and no animal stood a chance against a whole pack of these vicious killers.

Although Deinonychus was no taller than a human being, it carried an incredible amount of killing power.

HUNTING SKILLS

Its hind limbs were equipped with long, vicious claws that were capable of hanging onto and ripping open the flesh of the largest prey.

Before deciding our Top Ten Dinosaurs, we also considered these animals – all of them were deadly killers, but not quite deadly enough to make the Top Ten.

HERRERASAURUS

Herrerasaurus was one of the very first meat-eating **theropod** dinosaurs. It lived in South America about 225 million years ago during the **Triassic** period. Herrerasaurus was about three metres long and weighed about 200 kilograms. It walked and ran on its hind legs, and would have hunted small and medium-sized plant-eating dinosaurs, such as Pisanosaurus.

COELOPHYSIS

Coelophysis was a vicious pack-hunter that lived in North America during the late Triassic period. This small theropod dinosaur was about 3 metres long, but weighed just 25 kilograms. Hundreds of Coelophysis **fossils** were discovered at Ghost Ranch in New Mexico, USA, in the 1940s. Analysis of the fossils revealed that Coelophysis was a cannibal that sometimes ate its own kind.

BARYONYX

Baryonyx was a slightly smaller relative of Spinosaurus that lived in Europe and Africa about 120 million years ago. It measured about 10 metres in length and weighed about 2,000 kilograms. Like its larger relative, Baryonyx was a bipedal dinosaur that probably specialised in hunting fish, snatching them out of the water with its long jaws.

COMPSOGNATHUS

Compsognathus was one of the smallest known dinosaurs. It measured just 90 centimetres long and most of the length was in the tail. That did not stop it from being an agile and efficient predator. This tiny theropod was only about the size of a chicken and lived during the middle of the Jurassic period. Compsognathus was bipedal, and used the claws on its forefeet to hold its prey while it bit off chunks of flesh.

STRUTHIOMIMUS

This fast, bipedal **omnivore** lived in North America about 75 million years ago. Its name means "ostrich mimic" and like the present-day ostrich, this theropod dinosaur ate anything that it could find. Struthiomimus had large eyes at the sides of its head, and was constantly on the alert for danger. When threatened by larger predators, Struthiomimus could run away at speeds of up to 64 kph.

NO. 10 DILOPHOSAURUS

Dinosaur type	*Theropod*	**Extreme Scores**	
Fossil location	*North America*	**Body mass**	3
Size	*6 m*	**Mobility**	7
Lived when	*190 million years ago*	**Jaw power**	1
Discovered by	*Samuel Welles*	**Hunting skills**	4
Notable feature	*Head crest*	**Fright factor**	3

TOTAL SCORE 18 / 50

NO. 9 VELOCIRAPTOR

Dinosaur type	*Theropod*	**Extreme Scores**	
Fossil location	*Asia*	**Body mass**	1
Size	*60 cm*	**Mobility**	10
Lived when	*70 million years ago*	**Jaw power**	2
Discovered by	*Henry Osborn*	**Hunting skills**	8
Notable feature	*80 teeth*	**Fright factor**	1

TOTAL SCORE 22 / 50

NO. 8 GIGANOTOSAURUS

Dinosaur type	*Theropod*	**Extreme Scores**	
Fossil location	*South America*	**Body mass**	10
Size	*16 m*	**Mobility**	1
Lived when	*110 million years ago*	**Jaw power**	5
Discovered by	*Ruben Carolini*	**Hunting skills**	1
Notable feature	*2 metre skull*	**Fright factor**	6

TOTAL SCORE 23 / 50

NO. 7 TROODON

Dinosaur type	*Theropod*	**Extreme Scores**	
Fossil location	*North America*	**Body mass**	2
Size	*2 m*	**Mobility**	9
Lived when	*65 million years ago*	**Jaw power**	3
Discovered by	*Joseph Leidy*	**Hunting skills**	9
Notable feature	*Intelligence*	**Fright factor**	2

TOTAL SCORE 25 / 50

NO. 6 CARCHARODONTOSAURUS

Dinosaur type	*Theropod*	**Extreme Scores**	
Fossil location	*Africa*	**Body mass**	9
Size	*15 m*	**Mobility**	2
Lived when	*100 million years ago*	**Jaw power**	4
Discovered by	*Dr Stromer*	**Hunting skills**	2
Notable feature	*2 metre jaws*	**Fright factor**	9

TOTAL SCORE 26 / 50

NO. 5 ALBERTOSAURUS

		Extreme Scores	
Dinosaur type	*Theropod*	**Body mass**	5
Fossil location	*North America*	**Mobility**	6
Size	*8 m*	**Jaw power**	8
Lived when	*75 million years ago*	**Hunting skills**	5
Discovered by	*Joseph Tyrell*	**Fright factor**	4
Notable Feature	*Bulk and speed*		

TOTAL SCORE **28** / 50

NO. 4 ALLOSAURUS

		Extreme Scores	
Dinosaur type	*Theropod*	**Body mass**	6
Fossil location	*North America*	**Mobility**	4
Size	*12 m*	**Jaw power**	9
Lived when	*150 million years ago*	**Hunting skills**	7
Discovered by	*Othniel C Marsh*	**Fright factor**	5
Notable Feature	*Aggression*		

TOTAL SCORE **31** / 50

NO. 3 SPINOSAURUS

		Extreme Scores	
Dinosaur type	*Theropod*	**Body mass**	7
Fossil location	*Africa*	**Mobility**	5
Size	*15 m*	**Jaw power**	6
Lived when	*80 million years ago*	**Hunting skills**	6
Discovered by	*Ernst Stromer*	**Fright factor**	8
Notable Feature	*Long jaws*		

TOTAL SCORE **32** / 50

NO. 2 TYRANNOSAURUS REX

		Extreme Scores	
Dinosaur type	*Theropod*	**Body mass**	8
Fossil location	*North America*	**Mobility**	3
Size	*12 m*	**Jaw power**	10
Lived when	*65 million years ago*	**Hunting skills**	3
Discovered by	*Barnum Brown*	**Fright factor**	10
Notable Feature	*Jaw muscles*		

TOTAL SCORE **34** / 50

NO. 1 DEINONYCHUS

		Extreme Scores	
Dinosaur type	*Theropod*	**Body mass**	4
Fossil location	*North America*	**Mobility**	8
Size	*2 m*	**Jaw power**	7
Lived when	*100 million years ago*	**Hunting skills**	10
Discovered by	*Barnum Brown*	**Fright factor**	7
Notable Feature	*Ripping claws*		

TOTAL SCORE **36** / 50

This section is a catalogue of the most impressive of the ancient beasts that lived after the dinosaurs were wiped out some 65 million years ago. The sudden disappearance of the dinosaurs created numerous opportunities for the birds and mammals that survived the collision. Some of them grew larger, stronger, and fiercer than any mammals or birds before or since. We have rated these ancient beasts according to:

FIGHTING SKILLS

All animals are either predators or prey, and they all need effective fighting skills in order to survive. Predators obviously scored highly here, but we also found some herbivores capable of putting up a ferocious defence. Points were awarded for teeth, **tusks**, claws, and potential kicking power.

NO.9 MACRAUCHENIA

Macrauchenia was a very strange, long-necked mammal that had a short, muscular trunk. It lived in South America, where it fed on leaves and other kinds of plant food. The famous scientist Charles Darwin discovered the first fossils of Macrauchenia in the 1830s during his voyage around the world on the ship *Beagle*.

BODY MASS
Apart from the strange trunk, Macrauchenia looked rather like a camel, but without the hump. Its front legs were about 3 metres long. Its name means "long llama".

SKULL SIZE
Its skull was fairly small. The strange arrangement of the openings in the skull – the nostrils are located between the eyes – enabled scientists to work out that Macrauchenia had an elephant-like trunk.

FIGHTING SKILLS
This plant-eating mammal was not equipped for a fight – it had no horns, tusks, claws or sharp teeth. Its only hope was to run faster than the predators.

8

BODY MASS

In this category we gave the most points to animals with the greatest weight. In cases where there is not enough fossil evidence for an accurate estimate of an animal's weight, we took note of its height or length instead.

SKULL SIZE

Skull size tends to be a good indicator of an animal's comparative success, and we awarded points accordingly. A large skull usually means large jaws or a large beak, which allows the animal to feed more efficiently. A larger skull also provides room for larger eyes; and it may also accommodate a larger brain, although this is by no means always the case.

SPEED

Both predators and prey benefit from being able to move quickly, but speed alone is not everything. There is no point in being able to run (or swim) faster than your prey, if you cannot change direction easily, or come to a sudden stop. Our ancient beasts were given points for their speed, acceleration, and overall agility.

Despite its ungainly appearance, Macrauchenia was a fast and agile runner.

SPEED

The arrangements of the bones and joints in the lower part of the legs indicate to scientists that Macrauchenia was able to change direction at high-speed when being chased by a predator.

EXISTED FOR

It lived mainly during the Pliocene period, but only became extinct about 20,000 years ago.

The reconstructed skeleton of Macrauchenia illustrate a stooped stance.

EXTREME SCORES

It might not mean you any harm, but Macrauchenia could kick you out of the way without even noticing you.

BODY MASS 8/10

SKULL 4/10

FIGHTING SKILLS 2/10

SPEED 8/10

EXISTED FOR 5/10

= TOTAL SCORE

EXISTED FOR

All the animals in this book are extinct — they died out at some time in the past. We gave points according to how long ago these ancient beasts lived, the estimated longevity of individuals, and the length of time that the species survived. Extra points were given to those animals that lived in extreme conditions (e.g. during the **Ice Age**).

GASTORNIS

Gastornis was a large, flightless bird that lived not long after the land-living dinosaurs died out. It lived in the forests of Europe, where it may have hunted small mammals, using its huge beak to seize its prey. French scientist Gaston Planté discovered fossils of Gastornis in 1855 near Paris, France.

SKULL SIZE

The back half of the skull was fairly normal, but the front half, with the huge beak, was enormous. The beak itself was three times bigger than the rest of the skull put together.

Gastornis raided the nests of mammals and other birds.

FIGHTING SKILLS

Scientists cannot decide whether Gastornis was a plant-eater that used its beak for cracking nuts; or a carnivore that used its beak to rip open its prey. If attacked, Gastornis would have kicked out with the sharp claws on its feet.

SPEED

Gastornis had small, stumpy wings and could not fly. It had little use for high-speed movement because it lived in thick forests where running was difficult.

BODY MASS

Gastornis stood about 1.75 metres tall. Although it was shorter than a present-day ostrich, it was more heavily built.

Gastornis used its beak to tear up prey that was too big to swallow whole.

EXISTED FOR

Gastornis lived near the beginning of the **Tertiary** period, about 55 million years ago.

EXTREME SCORES

A big bird with a massive beak and a taste for the flesh of mammals – it would not make a nice pet.

BODY MASS
3/10

SKULL SIZE
5/10

FIGHTING SKILLS
6/10

SPEED
6/10

EXISTED FOR
6/10

= TOTAL SCORE

2?/50

MACRAUCHENIA

Macrauchenia was a very strange, long-necked mammal that had a short, muscular trunk. It lived in South America, where it fed on leaves and other kinds of plant food. The famous scientist Charles Darwin discovered the first fossils of Macrauchenia in the 1830s during his voyage around the world on the ship *Beagle*.

BODY MASS

Apart from the strange trunk, Macrauchenia looked rather like a camel, but without the hump. Its front legs were about 3 metres long. Its name means "long llama".

SKULL SIZE

Its skull was fairly small. The strange arrangement of the openings in the skull – the **nostrils** are located between the eyes – enabled scientists to work out that Macrauchenia had an elephant-like trunk.

FIGHTING SKILLS

This plant-eating mammal was not equipped for a fight – it had no horns, tusks, claws or sharp teeth. Its only hope was to run faster than the predators.

Despite its ungainly appearance, Macrauchenia was a fast and agile runner.

SPEED

The arrangements of the bones and **joints** in the lower part of the legs indicate to scientists that Macrauchenia was able to change direction at high-speed when being chased by a predator.

EXISTED FOR

It lived mainly during the **Pliocene** epoch, but only became extinct about 20,000 years ago.

It might not mean you any harm, but Macrauchenia could kick you out of the way without even noticing you.

BODY MASS
8/10

SKULL SIZE
4/10

FIGHTING SKILLS
2/10

SPEED
8/10

EXISTED FOR
5/10

= TOTAL SCORE

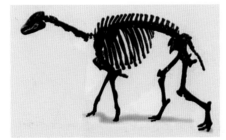

The reconstructed skeleton of Macrauchenia illustrates a stooped stance.

Sabre-toothed cats were fierce and deadly ice-age carnivores. Species such as Smilodon in North America and Homotherium in Africa were the top predators of all they surveyed. Some of the finest sabre-toothed fossils are those of Smilodon that were discovered in the La Brea tar pits in California, USA.

BODY MASS

These beasts were about the same size as present-day big cats, and weighed about 200 kilograms.

SKULL SIZE

A sabre-toothed cat had a skull about 30 centimetres long, with two canine teeth projecting down from the front of its upper **jaw**.

FIGHTING SKILLS

Sabre-toothed cats were ambush hunters. These cats probably used their long teeth for slashing at the vulnerable undersides of their prey.

Sabre-toothed cats used their teeth to attack the soft belly of their prey.

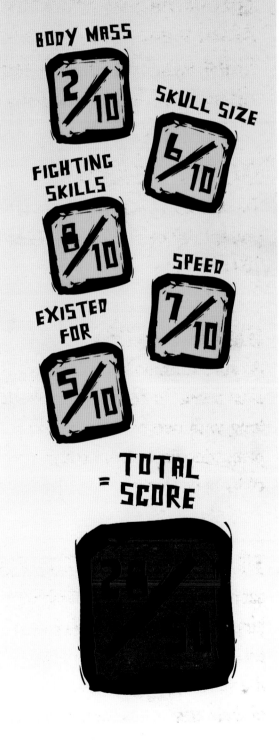

The other teeth are tiny in comparison to the two "sabres".

SPEED

They had shorter legs than other big cats, and were not designed for speed. They could only run over very short distances.

EXISTED FOR

The sabre-toothed cats lived during the Pliocene **epoch**.

A ferocious hunter with the longest cutting teeth of any mammal, this was not a cute little kitty!

BODY MASS
2/10

SKULL SIZE
6/10

FIGHTING SKILLS
8/10

SPEED
7/10

EXISTED FOR
5/10

= TOTAL SCORE

Andrewsarchus is the largest meat-eating land mammal so far discovered. It looked like a cross between a tiger and a wolf, but it was neither a cat nor a dog – it was most closely related to the toothed whales. Andrewsarchus lived in Asia near to lakes and rivers, and the first fossils were discovered in Mongolia by palaeontologist Kan Chuen Pao.

BODY MASS

It was a lot bigger than a polar bear. Andrewsarchus measured 5 metres in length (excluding the tail), and weighed about 1,000 kilograms.

SKULL SIZE

Andrewsarchus had a massive skull about 100 centimetres in length.

FIGHTING SKILLS

Andrewsarchus was not a very efficient hunter, and if it ate large animals they were probably carrion. It mainly hunted turtles and other small animals that it found near riverbanks.

Powerful jaws and strong teeth could easily crush turtle shells.

SPEED

Andrewsarchus was not built for long chases, and it most likely relied on stealth to take its prey by surprise.

This predator probably had spotted fur for **camouflage**.

EXISTED FOR

Andrewsarchus lived during the late **Eocene** epoch, about 42-37 million years ago.

EXTREME SCORES

The biggest-ever meat-eating mammal – Andrewsarchus was larger than a family car and had sharper teeth.

BODY MASS
4/10

SKULL SIZE
7/10

FIGHTING SKILLS
8/10

SPEED
3/10

EXISTED FOR
7/10

= TOTAL SCORE

CHALICOTHERES

The chalicotheres are one of the most puzzling groups of ancient beasts. They lived during the period, and were widespread in Asia, Europe, North Africa and North America. Chalicotheres had forelegs that were much longer than their hind legs, and strange elongated heads – their nearest living relatives are horses.

BODY MASS

Most chalicotheres ranged in size from goat to gorilla – the largest stood about 3 metres tall.

SKULL SIZE

The large, elongated skull is the chalicothere's most horse-like feature. The jaws had chewing teeth at the back, but no front teeth.

FIGHTING SKILLS

The long front legs gave it a good reach, but the claws were designed for digging up roots or dragging down branches, and were not much use in a fight.

This jaw bone found in agate fossil beds near Nebraska, United States.

Large, ugly and probably very smelly, chalicotheres would not make good dancing partners.

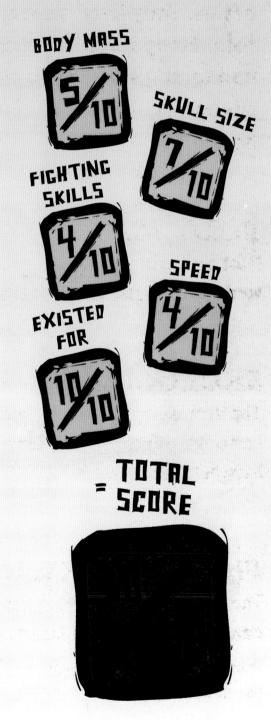

BODY MASS
5/10

SKULL SIZE
7/10

FIGHTING SKILLS
4/10

SPEED
4/10

EXISTED FOR
10/10

= TOTAL SCORE

SPEED

Chalicothere was a bulky, clumsy beast that probably tried to climb trees to escape from danger rather than run away.

EXISTED FOR

Chalicothere lived during the whole of the Eocene from 53–37 million years ago.

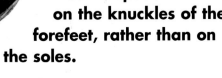

Some species walked on the knuckles of their forefeet, rather than on the soles.

AMBULOCETUS

Ambulocetus was a medium-sized predator that was equally at home in water or on land. This meat-eating mammal could tackle prey much larger than its own size. Ambulocetus lived in Asia and Africa about 50 million years ago. The first fossils of Ambulocetus were discovered in Pakistan.

BODY MASS

It had a total length of about 3 metres, including the tail, and weighed about 300 kilograms.

SKULL SIZE

Ambulocetus was one of the earliest whales, and it had an elongated skull with rows of sharp teeth.

FIGHTING SKILLS

Its legs were fairly weak and its claws useless for fighting, but its powerful jaws and sharp teeth were a fearsome weapon.

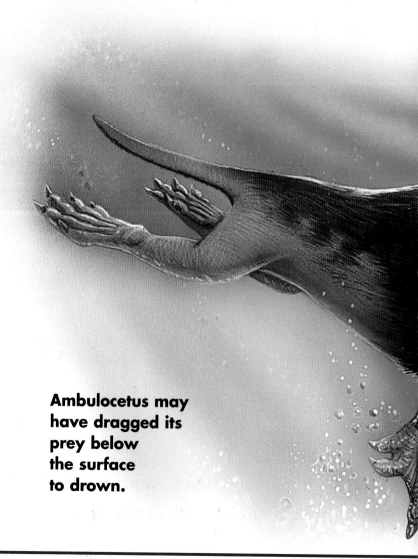

Ambulocetus may have dragged its prey below the surface to drown.

Its overall shape was rather like a crocodile.

SPEED

It was fairly slow on land, but faster in the water, where it could use its feet as paddles.

EXISTED FOR

Ambulocetus lived during the early part of the Eocene epoch, about 58-40 million years ago.

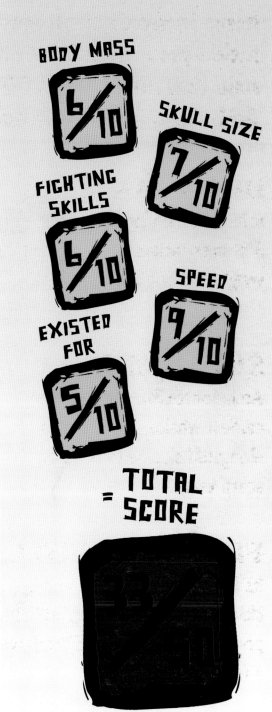

Its name means "walking whale" – it was a killer whale with four legs.

BODY MASS
6/10

SKULL SIZE
7/10

FIGHTING SKILLS
6/10

SPEED
9/10

EXISTED FOR
5/10

= TOTAL SCORE

INDRICOTHERE

Indricothere is the largest land mammal that has ever lived on Earth. This giant herbivore once lived in southern Asia. It was taller than a present-day giraffe, and was much more heavily built. Despite its long-necked appearance, the nearest living relative of Indricothere is the rhinoceros.

BODY MASS

Indricothere stood up to 8 metres tall and weighed more than 15,000 kilograms. They were bigger than the largest members of the elephant family, but not as large as whales.

SKULL SIZE

Compared with the rest of its body, Indricotherium's skull was small and lightweight. The male would have had a larger and more domed skull than the female.

FIGHTING SKILLS

Its great size was probably its best defence, and even a predator such as Andrewsarchus would have been wary of a kick from one of its massive feet.

Indricotheres probably lived in family groups like elephants do today.

SPEED

Indricothere ate leaves from branches high above the ground so they had no need to move quickly to catch prey. Its bulk meant it faced few predators.

EXISTED FOR

This massive mammal lived during the **Oligocene** epoch, about 35 million years ago.

Indricotherium is the largest mammal that ever walked the Earth.

If you ventured too close, you would be in danger of being trodden flat by this immense mammal.

BODY MASS
10/10

SKULL SIZE
8/10

FIGHTING SKILLS
6/10

SPEED
3/10

EXISTED FOR
7/10

= TOTAL SCORE

Mammoths were shaggy, fur-covered relatives of the elephant that lived during the Ice Age. There were several species of large mammoths that lived in Europe, Asia and North America, and some of them had very long tusks. There were also dwarf mammoths living on islands near the coast of California.

BODY MASS

The Columbian mammoth of North America was one of the largest species and measured more than 4 metres tall. A fully-grown adult weighed about 10,000 kilograms.

All mammoths had a hump behind the head like present-day Asian elephants.

SKULL SIZE

The skull was large and strongly built to provide a firm anchorage for the huge ivory tusks. The chewing teeth were also very large.

The massive chewing teeth had surfaces designed for grinding up vegetation.

FIGHTING SKILL

The tusks were the main weapon and were used for fighting other mammoths as well as for defence against predators.

SPEED

Like modern elephants, mammoths could run quite quickly when they wanted to.

EXISTED FOR

Mammoths lived during the Pliocene Ice Age, and only became extinct about 15,000 years ago.

If this hairy beast did not spear you with its tusks, it would trample you underfoot.

BODY MASS
9/10

SKULL SIZE
10/10

FIGHTING SKILLS
6/10

SPEED
5/10

EXISTED FOR
5/10

= TOTAL SCORE
35/50

Phorusrhacos was one of the biggest and fiercest birds that ever walked the Earth. It was a deadly predator, and is sometimes known as the "terror bird". Phorusrhacos could attack and eat prey that were as large as a camel. It lived in South America about 20 million years ago.

BODY MASS

Phorusrhacos stood about 2.5 metres tall and was heavy for a bird, much too heavy to fly – it weighed up to 150 kilograms.

FIGHTING SKILLS

Its beak was strong enough to snap the spine of an animal the size of a wolf, and it would attack much larger prey.

SKULL SIZE

The skull of Phorusrhacos was about 65 centimetres long, and more than half of this consisted of the deadly curving beak.

Like many of the early birds, Phorusrhacos had claws on its wings as well as its feet.

The strong skull and powerful beak of a dedicated predator.

At the time Phorusrhacos was the fastest thing on two legs, and few animals could escape its deadly beak.

BODY MASS
5/10

SKULL SIZE
7/10

FIGHTING SKILLS
6/10

SPEED
10/10

EXISTED FOR
9/10

= **TOTAL SCORE**
37/50

SPEED

Phorusrhacos had tiny wings and could not fly, but it was a fast runner that could outrun most of its prey. It was also strong enough to chase prey over long distances.

EXISTED FOR

Phorusrhacos lived during the **Miocene** epoch, about 20 million years ago.

Imagine a ferocious and wild giant pig with powerful jaws and long, pointed teeth – that is Entelodon, our overall winner. Entelodon was neither a carnivore nor a herbivore; it was an omnivore that ate anything that came along. Its jaws were so powerful that it could crunch up the skulls of other animals.

BODY MASS

Entelodon was about the size of a buffalo. It weighed more than 1,000 kilograms.

SKULL SIZE

The skull was massive, and the jaws were long and wide with lots of large teeth.

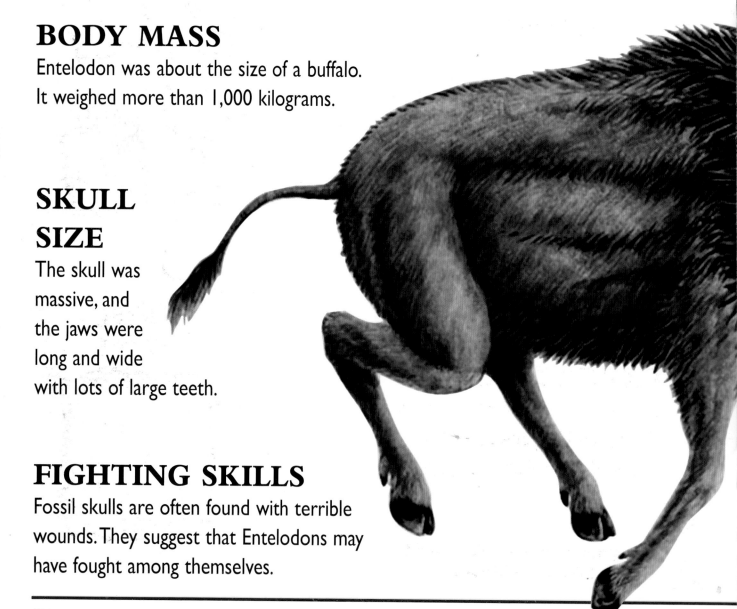

FIGHTING SKILLS

Fossil skulls are often found with terrible wounds. They suggest that Entelodons may have fought among themselves.

These massive jaws could snap a leg as easily as breaking a twig.

SPEED

Entelodon was a fast runner, but it mainly used its speed to escape from danger, and did not chase after its prey.

EXISTED FOR

Entelodon lived in North America during the **Oligocene** epoch, about 35-25 million years ago.

This giant relative of pigs would eat anything it could find.

EXTREME SCORES

Large, powerful, and highly unpredictable – Entelodon was one of the most dangerous beasts of all time.

BODY MASS
7/10

SKULL SIZE
9/10

FIGHTING SKILLS
10/10

SPEED
7/10

EXISTED FOR
8/10

= TOTAL SCORE

CLOSE
BUT NOT CLOSE ENOUGH

Choosing just ten ancient beasts for this section was very difficult. Here are five beasts that didn't quite make the final list...

DESMOSTYLIANS

The desmostylians were a very strange group of mammals that lived about 35 million years ago. They were about the same size as present-day horses, and lived in shallow water along coastlines. They may have walked along the seabed, while using their peculiar teeth to dig out shellfish. The desmostylians were not closely related to any of the mammals that exist today.

MEGATHERIUM

Megatherium was a gigantic, shaggy-haired ground sloth that only became extinct about 10,000 years ago. This mammal lived in South America, and grew to more than 6 metres in length. Megatherium was a herbivore that fed mainly on the leaves and shoots of trees. It walked on all fours, but could stand up on its hind legs to reach the higher branches. It was hunted by sabre-toothed cats.

ARSINOITHERIUM

Arsinoitherium was a horned mammal that lived in Africa about 35 million years ago. Despite its appearance, it was not related to the present-day rhinoceros. The twin horns of Arsinoitherium were made of bone and were a part of the animal's skull. The horn of a rhinoceros, however, is not part of the skull and it is made from tightly compressed hair.

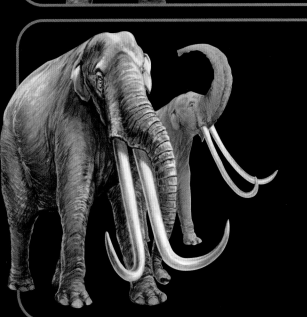

STEGODON

Stegodon lived in Africa and Asia about 10-12 million years ago. It was related to mammoths and present-day elephants, and had the same long trunk, but its tusks tended to be longer and much straighter. The longest fossil Stegodon tusks that have so far been discovered were each more than 3 metres in length.

BULLOCKORNIS

Bullockornis was a giant duck that lived in Australia about 20 million years ago. It had long, powerful legs and stood about 3 metres tall. Although Bullockornis was a kind of duck, it did not have a flat duck's bill. Instead, it had a large, curved beak that was most likely used to tear strips of flesh from the carcasses of dead animals.

NO. 10 GASTORNIS

Animal type	Bird
Fossil location	Europe
Food	Carnivore
Living relatives	Hoatzin
Discovered by	Gaston Planté
Notable feature	Enormous beak

Extreme Scores — TOTAL SCORE **26 / 50**

Body Mass	3
Skull Size	5
Fighting Skills	6
Speed	6
Existed for	6

NO. 9 MACRAUCHENIA

Animal type	Mammal
Fossil location	South America
Food	Herbivore
Living relatives	none
Discovered by	Charles Darwin
Notable feature	Running speed

Extreme Scores — TOTAL SCORE **27 / 50**

Body Mass	8
Skull Size	4
Fighting Skills	2
Speed	8
Existed for	5

NO. 8 SABRE-TOOTHED CATS

Animal type	Mammal
Fossil location	Africa, North America
Food	Carnivore
Living relatives	Tiger
Discovered by	L Anderson
Notable feature	Dagger-like teeth

Extreme Scores — TOTAL SCORE **28 / 50**

Body Mass	2
Skull Size	6
Fighting Skills	8
Speed	7
Existed for	5

NO. 7 ANDREWSARCHUS

Animal type	Mammal
Fossil location	Asia
Food	Carnivore
Living relatives	Killer Whale
Discovered by	Kan Chuen Pao
Notable feature	Massive skull

Extreme Scores — TOTAL SCORE **29 / 50**

Body Mass	4
Skull Size	7
Fighting Skills	8
Speed	3
Existed for	7

NO. 6 CHALICOTHERES

Animal type	Mammal
Fossil location	Europe, Asia, Africa, North America
Food	Herbivore
Living relatives	Horses
Discovered by	Forsyth Major
Notable feature	Long front legs

Extreme Scores — TOTAL SCORE **30 / 50**

Body Mass	5
Skull Size	7
Fighting Skills	4
Speed	4
Existed for	10

NO. 5 AMBULOCETUS

		Extreme Scores	TOTAL SCORE
Animal type:	Mammal		
Fossil location:	Asia, Africa	Body Mass	6
Food:	Carnivore	Skull Size	7
Living relatives:	Killer Whale	Fighting Skills	6
Discovered by:	Hans Thewissen	Speed	9
Notable feature:	Powerful jaws	Existed for	5

TOTAL SCORE **33**/50

NO. 4 INDRICOTHERE

		Extreme Scores	TOTAL SCORE
Animal type	Mammal		
Fossil location	Asia	Body Mass	10
Food	Herbivore	Skull Size	8
Living relatives	Rhinoceros	Fighting Skills	6
Discovered by	C. Forster Cooper	Speed	3
Notable feature	Great size	Existed for	7

TOTAL SCORE **34**/50

NO. 3 MAMMOTH

		Extreme Scores	TOTAL SCORE
Animal type:	Mammal		
Fossil location	North America	Body Mass	9
Food	Herbivore	Skull Size	10
Living relatives	Asian Elephants	Fighting Skills	6
Discovered by	Unknown	Speed	5
Notable feature	Ivory tusks	Existed for	5

TOTAL SCORE **35**/50

NO. 2 PHORSRHACOS

		Extreme Scores	TOTAL SCORE
Animal type	Bird		
Fossil location	South America	Body Mass	5
Food	Carnivore	Skull Size	7
Living relatives	Parrots	Fighting Skills	6
Discovered by	Benjamin Waller	Speed	10
Notable feature	Powerful beak	Existed for	9

TOTAL SCORE **37**/50

NO. 1 ENTELODON

		Extreme Scores	TOTAL SCORE
Animal type	Mammal		
Fossil location	North America	Body Mass	7
Food	Omivore	Skull Size	9
Living relatives	Wild pigs	Fighting Skills	10
Discovered by	Gaston Plante	Speed	7
Notable feature	Bone-crunching jaws	Existed for	8

TOTAL SCORE **41**/50

This section is a catalogue of the world's most deadly living creatures. There are lots and lots of dangerous animals around the world, and many of these can cause injury, and even death. But most of them are just dangerous because they are large or have sharp teeth. The creatures in this book are different – they are not just dangerous, they are killers one and all. Our top ten deadly creatures were rated according to:

SHAPE

When studying deadly creatures, it soon became clear that size was not particularly important. Instead, we gave points for complexity of shape – the animals with the most complex shapes were awarded the most points. A more complicated shape can make a creature difficult to recognize and avoid. Its shape may also give the creature an increased opportunity for attack.

NO.9 — SYDNEY FUNNEL-WEB SPIDER

The funnel-web spider that lives around the city of Sydney in Australia is probably the most dangerous spider on earth. Although it mainly lives in the woodland surrounding the city, the Sydney funnel-web spider is often found in garages and backyards, and even underneath the floors of houses.

SHAPE
The Sydney funnel-web is quite large for a spider, with a body length of about2-4 centimetres. Males are more lightly built than females.

DANGER
Most spiders have **venom** that is too weak to affect large animals. The Sydney funnel-web spider is unusual because its venom is super-deadly to human beings, and its **jaws** can bite through clothing.

The Sydney funnel-web spider injects its venom through a pair of sharp, curved fangs.

ATTACK
This spider is an active hunter that wanders over the ground at night in search of prey. When threatened, it raises its head and forelegs before delivering its deadly bite.

60

DANGER

For this category we looked at all the features that make a particular animal dangerous, and gave them separate scores. We also considered whether the animal is aggressive (which increases its danger score), how widely it is distributed, and whether it is common or rare. The overall score is a combination of all these factors.

ATTACK

Here we examined the actual process of the animal's attack, and the mechanisms it uses to kill its victims. Animals that used an unusual method of attack were scored more highly than those that share their method of attack with many other creatures. Additional points were given to those deadly creatures that take their victims by surprise.

LETHAL

This category is only concerned with the physical effects of the venom, **toxin** or other substance that causes death. Wherever possible, records of attacks on human beings were examined, and the lethality of the substance expressed in terms of human deaths. The effects on any intended prey, which is generally much smaller than a human being, can be considered as the same.

Funnel webs are dark brown in colour, and live in funnel-shaped retreats.

EXTREME SCORES

A spider with sharp fangs, deadly venom, and a reputation for being bad-tempered. Beware!

SHAPE
8/10

DANGER
4/10

ATTACK
4/10

LETHAL
3/10

PREY
5/10

= TOTAL SCORE

LETHAL

The Sydney funnel-web spider has its own unique venom. Once it gets into the bloodstream it begins to attack the heart and can cause death in less than one hour.

PREY

This spider will attack humans if it feels threatened, but it mainly eats snails, slugs and small **amphibians**, beetles, and cockroaches. They even eat small lizards.

61

PREY

Here, the focus is on what these deadly creatures eat – even if, as with the stonefish, they do not actually use their deadly characteristics while hunting. We looked at the size and variety of prey, and we also considered whether the prey was easy or difficult to locate.

POISON DART FROG

Most people think that small frogs are harmless, but the poison dart frog will soon make them change their minds. The poison dart froglives in the **tropical rain forests** of Central and South America. Native people sometimes smear the frog's poison on the tips of their arrows and blowpipe darts when they go hunting.

SHAPE

The poison dart frog ranges in size from just over 2 centimetres (the Strawberry Poison Dart Frog) to 8 centimetres (Dyeing Poison Frog).

DANGER

This small **amphibian** uses poison as a defence mechanism. Their bright colours warn predators that these frogs are definitely not good to eat.

ATTACK

A thin layer of deadly poisonous slime covers the poison dart frog. The slime oozes from small **glands** in the frog's skin.

The frog's bright coloration is a vivid warning: do not touch!

LETHAL

The glands produce a toxin that stops muscles from working and causes death. Just touching a poison frog can transfer enough toxin to kill an adult human being.

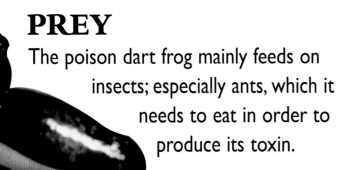

PREY

The poison dart frog mainly feeds on insects; especially ants, which it needs to eat in order to produce its toxin.

The skin of the poison dart frog is coated with poisonous slime.

This frog is small, attractive and deadly. If you see one, do not be tempted to touch it.

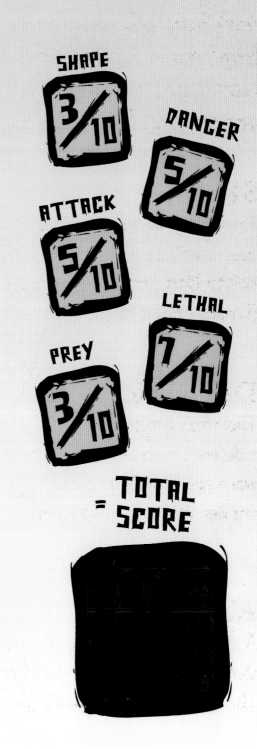

SHAPE
3/10

DANGER
5/10

ATTACK
5/10

LETHAL
7/10

PREY
3/10

= TOTAL SCORE

SYDNEY FUNNEL-WEB SPIDER

The funnel-web spider that lives around the city of Sydney in Australia is probably the most dangerous spider on Earth. Although it mainly lives in the woodland surrounding the city, the Sydney funnel-web spider is often found in garages and backyards, and even underneath the floors of houses.

SHAPE

The Sydney funnel-web is quite large for a spider, with a body length of about 2-4 centimetres. Males are more lightly built than females.

The Sydney funnel-web spider injects its venom through a huge pair of sharp, curved fangs.

DANGER

Most spiders have venom that is too weak to affect large animals. The Sydney funnel-web spider is unusual because its venom is super-deadly to human beings, and its jaws can bite through clothing.

ATTACK

This spider is an active hunter that wanders over the ground at night in search of prey. When threatened, it raises its head and forelegs before delivering its deadly bite.

Funnel webs are dark brown in colour,
and live in funnel-shaped retreats.

LETHAL

The Sydney funnel-web spider has its
own unique venom. Once it gets into the
bloodstream it begins to attack the
heart and can cause death
in less than one hour.

PREY

This spider will attack humans if
it feels threatened, but it mainly eats
snails, slugs and small **amphibians**,
beetles, and cockroaches. They even
eat small lizards.

A spider with sharp fangs, deadly venom,
and a reputation for being bad-
tempered. Beware!

SHAPE
8/10

DANGER
4/10

ATTACK
4/10

LETHAL
3/10

PREY
5/10

= **TOTAL SCORE**

BLUE-RINGED OCTOPUS

The blue-ringed octopus is one of the most beautiful of all sea creatures – it is also one of the most deadly. This small, shy animal lives around **coral reefs** in the Indian and Pacific Oceans. Swimmers and divers have learned not to go looking for this octopus because it has a very nasty bite.

SHAPE

Like all octopi, this one has a soft body with eight arms. The blue-ringed octopus is only about 10 centimetres long – about the size of a tennis ball.

DANGER

The blue-ringed octopus is the only octopus that has a venomous bite. People swimming in the sea that accidentally disturb this octopus are likely to get bitten with lethal results.

ATTACK

The octopus has a sharp beak that can slice into flesh. This allows its venomous **saliva** to flow into the wound.

A beautiful but deadly animal that is active during the day, which is when most people go swimming – make sure you take care in the water!

SHAPE
6/10

DANGER
5/10

ATTACK
6/10

LETHAL
5/10

PREY
6/10

= TOTAL SCORE

A blue-ringed octopus weighs about 30 grams.

LETHAL

At first the bite feels like a bee-sting. Then the victim goes numb and dies. There is no known **antidote** for blue-ringed octopus venom.

PREY

This octopus feeds mainly on crabs, and wounded fish that cannot swim away quickly.

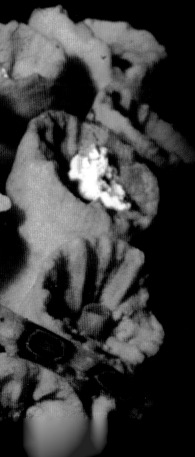

The blue rings are a warning that the octopus is angry or frightened – in either case it may bite.

STONEFISH

Meet the fish that looks just like a rock – the stonefish, which lives around the coasts of the Indian and Pacific Oceans. Not only is it very ugly, it is also very dangerous, because the stonefish is the most **venomous** fish in the sea. Its sharp spines can easily penetrate flesh and inject their deadly venom.

SHAPE

A stonefish can grow up to 50 centimetres in length, with lumpy skin as camouflage that helps disguise its shape.

DANGER

The stonefish likes to lie half buried on the seabed waiting in ambush for its prey. People paddling or swimming in the sea sometimes step on a camouflaged stonefish by mistake.

A stonefish does not swim away when disturbed, it turns to face the intruder.

ATTACK

There are 13 sharp, hollow spines in the fin running along the stonefish's back. Each of these spines can inject a deadly dose of venom.

LETHAL

If you step on a stonefish it will start to hurt straight away, and the pain will rapidly get worse. Some victims die within a few hours.

PREY

The stonefish only uses its spines for defence. It waits for shrimp and small fish to pass by, then strikes, gulping them down in under a second.

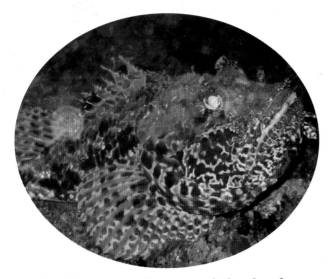

The fin along the stonefish's back contains no less than 13 nasty surprises.

Spines full of deadly venom hidden on a camouflaged fish – make sure that the next stone you step on really is a stone and not a stonefish.

SHAPE
5/10

DANGER
7/10

ATTACK
7/10

LETHAL
5/10

PREY
5/10

= TOTAL SCORE

The Palestine scorpion is the most dangerous scorpion in the world. It is found in the **deserts** and scrubland of the Middle East and North Africa. The Palestine scorpion is so deadly that local people have given it the name "Deathstalker".

SHAPE

The Palestine Scorpion is about 8-11 centimetres long with two large **pincers** and a deadly tail **sting**.

DANGER

This monster often hides under rocks or among loose sand and stones. If disturbed it will lash out with its deadly tail. Children are often stung while playing or walking to and from school.

ATTACK

The sharp sting penetrates flesh and injects deadly venom. The Palestine scorpion will sometimes sting a victim over and over again.

The sting at the end the Deathstalker's curving tail carries a load of deadly venom.

Yellow coloration helps the
scorpion to hide in desert sand.

LETHAL

One drop of the venom is
enough to kill an animal much
larger than itself. Fortunately,
scientists have developed an
antidote for the sting of the
Palestine scorpion.

PREY

It hunts insects but
does not use its sting;
instead it tears its prey
apart with its pincers.

The Palestine scorpion lives up to its
nickname - "Deathstalker" – so stay
away from the desert.

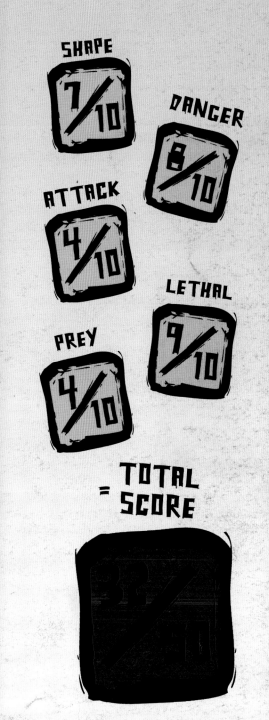

SHAPE
7/10

DANGER
8/10

ATTACK
4/10

LETHAL
9/10

PREY
4/10

= TOTAL SCORE

The Fierce Snake is not as famous as cobras and rattlesnakes, but it is a lot more deadly because it has the deadliest venom of any snake. The Fierce Snake, which is also known as the "Inland Taipan", is only found in central and northern Australia where it is very rare. The first live specimen was not captured until 1975.

SHAPE

The Fierce Snake grows up to 2.5 metres long. Its smooth body is brown in colour with a mustard-yellow belly and a glossy black head.

The Fierce Snake has enough deadly venom to kill 100 people.

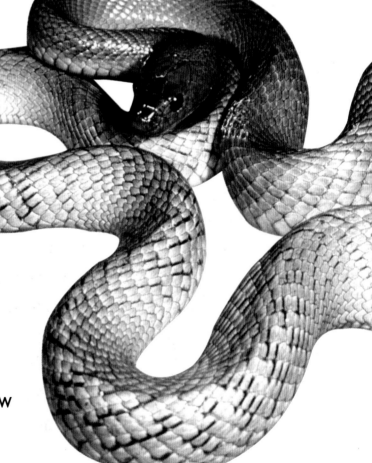

DANGER

The Fierce Snake is shy and rare and usually docile, but if you are unlucky enough to see one – walk slowly away, because it can be very aggressive if disturbed.

ATTACK

This snake can strike faster than the eye can follow. As it bites its victim, two hollow fangs inject a small dose of its venom.

Inside the mouth are two sharp fangs that inject venom into victims.

LETHAL

This creature has the most toxic venom of any snake. The Fierce Snake carries enough poison to kill about 250,000 mice, or about 100 adult humans.

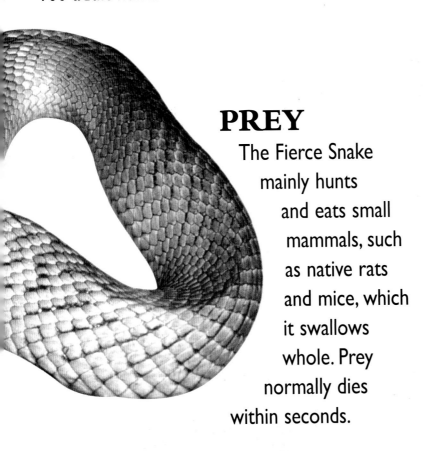

PREY

The Fierce Snake mainly hunts and eats small mammals, such as native rats and mice, which it swallows whole. Prey normally dies within seconds.

How can you rate the world's deadliest snake? Fortunately for us, the Fierce Snake is very rare.

SHAPE
6/10

DANGER
6/10

ATTACK
8/10

LETHAL
9/10

PREY
6/10

= TOTAL SCORE

"Mosquito" is a Portuguese word meaning little fly, and its use dates back to about 1583. The mosquito just wants to drink a little warm, human blood. But, while it drinks our blood, the Anopheles mosquito also gives us the deadly disease called **malaria**, and has killed more people than any other animal on our planet.

SHAPE

A mosquito has two scaled wings, a slender body, and six long legs. They can vary in size but are rarely larger than 15 millimetres.

DANGER

The Anopheles mosquito has a tiny **microbe** living in its body. When it sucks blood, the microbe leaks into the victim's bloodstream.
In human victims, this microbe causes the killer disease malaria.

ATTACK

A mosquito does not bite with teeth. It has a feeding tube like a hollow needle. It jabs this tube into human skin to suck up blood.

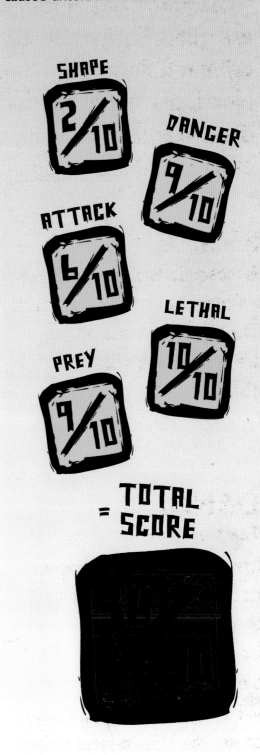

Female mosquitoes must drink
blood in order to lay eggs.

LETHAL

Taking a tiny amount of blood causes no
problem at all. But
malaria has killed
hundreds of millions
of people throughout
human history.

Each mosquito takes
just a tiny drop of
bright red blood.

PREY

Mosquitoes are only interested in drinking the
blood of mammals – humans are easy targets.
Mosquito adults also feed on flower nectar and
juices of fruits for flight energy.

Small and hard to see, the Anopheles
does not look like a killer, but it has
caused untold millions of human deaths.

SHAPE
2/10

DANGER
9/10

ATTACK
6/10

LETHAL
10/10

PREY
9/10

= TOTAL
SCORE

BEAKED SEA SNAKE

The Beaked Sea Snake lives in the Pacific Ocean area around Australia. This sea snake is a bad-tempered killer. This one species is responsible for about half of all sea snake attacks, and for 90 percent of deaths from sea snake bites. The venom of the Beaked Sea Snake is deadlier than that of most land snakes.

SHAPE

This snake can reach a length of up to 2 metres. They have specialised flattened tails for swimming and veils over their nostrils which are closed in water.

DANGER

The Beaked Sea Snake is often caught in fishing nets. People trying to take the snakes out of the nets are the ones most likely to get bitten. The Beaked Sea Snake is responsible for more than half of all cases of sea snake bites.

ATTACK

Sea snakes have much shorter fangs than land snakes – just 2-4 millimetres long but they are just as sharp and deadly. The venom of the Beaked Sea Snake acts very quickly.

The Beaked Sea Snake grows
to about 1.3 metres long.

LETHAL

The venom is the sixth most
deadly of any snake in the world.
It attacks the muscles and stops
the victim from breathing,
which quickly causes death.
Just one drop of venom is
enough to kill three men.

PREY

The Beaked Sea Snake can
swallow its **prey** twice the
size of its neck. This strange
snake's main diet is fish, fish
eggs and eels.

**Vivid black markings make this deadly
sea snake easy to identify.**

An aggressive and bad-tempered
animal with sharp fangs and deadly
venom – the Beaked Sea Snake would
certainly not make a good pet.

SHAPE
7/10

DANGER
8/10

ATTACK
8/10

LETHAL
8/10

PREY
6/10

= TOTAL SCORE

PIRANHA

This fish has earned its nickname of the "Wolf of the Waters". It has sharp teeth and hunts in groups – one piranha will give you a nasty bite, but a group of them will strip the flesh from your bones. The piranha is found in the Amazon and other rivers in South America.

SHAPE

The average length is about 30 centimetres, but a well-fed piranha can reach twice that size.

When piranhas are in a feeding frenzy, the water seems to churn and turns red with blood.

DANGER

The piranha has a superb sense of smell and can detect blood in the water from more than a mile away. It lives in **shoals** of 100 or so fish that can all attack at the same time.

ATTACK

Piranhas do not kill their prey, they just start eating it alive! Their teeth are triangular in shape and are razor sharp. When they have finished feeding, only the bones are left.

The teeth of the piranha are specialised flesh slicers.

LETHAL

They will attack anything – even human beings. Most victims die from loss of blood.

PREY

The piranha normally eats fish, crabs and small mammals, and can devour even large animals within minutes.

The flesh-eating piranha makes another good reason to stay out of the water – this fish will start eating unwary swimmers without any warning.

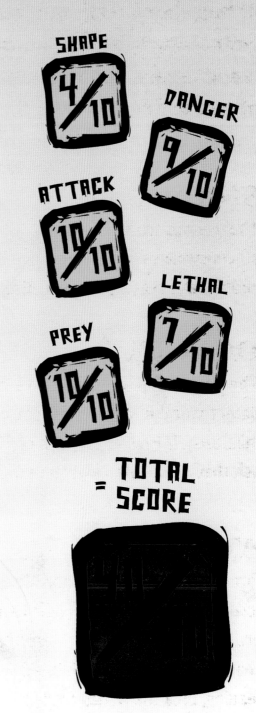

SHAPE
4/10

DANGER
9/10

ATTACK
10/10

LETHAL
7/10

PREY
10/10

= TOTAL SCORE

SEA WASP JELLYFISH

The final verdict – no living creature is more deadly than this jellyfish. This small, boneless animal is found in the seas around Australia. It has dozens of stinging **tentacles** armed with deadly venom that kills almost instantly. To make matters worse, the transparent and colourless sea wasp is almost impossible to see underwater.

SHAPE

It has a roughly four-sided shape (it is also known as the Box Jellyfish) and grows to about 30 centimetres in width, with tentacles that are more than 100 centimetres in length.

DANGER

Hundreds of people are stung every year, and many die. To protect people, many beaches in Australia are closed when there are Sea Wasps about.

PREY

The Sea Wasp feeds mainly on shrimp and small fish.

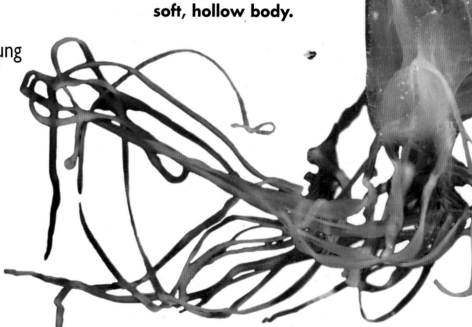

All jellyfish have a soft, hollow body.

The white blobs on the tentacles are clusters of tiny, spring-loaded stings.

ATTACK

Every tentacle has thousands of tiny, coiled stings, each one with a sharp point. These stings are triggered by the slightest touch and inject deadly venom into the victim.

LETHAL

Sea Wasp victims feel a sudden burning pain, and the venom may stop the heart from beating within a few minutes. A single Sea Wasp carries enough venom to kill about 50 human beings.

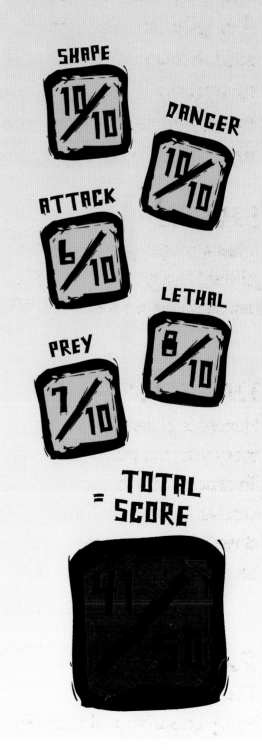

EXTREME SCORES

Not just deadly, this creature is almost impossible to see, which is more than enough reason to avoid it at all costs!

SHAPE
10/10

DANGER
10/10

ATTACK
6/10

LETHAL
8/10

PREY
7/10

= TOTAL SCORE

Before deciding our Top Ten Deadly Creatures, we also considered these animals - all of them are deadly killers, but not quite deadly enough to make the Top Ten.

CONE SHELL

The Cone Shell is a kind of **marine** gastropod (sea snail). Its shell is about 7-10 centimetres long, and it is often brightly coloured. If you saw one on a beach, you might be tempted to pick it up – bad move! All Cone Shells can inflict a painful sting, and some **species** also inject a deadly toxin.

GILA MONSTER

This strange-looking reptile is one of only two venomous lizards in the whole world – and they both live in the deserts of the southwestern USA, and northern Mexico. The Gila monster does not have two long fangs to injects its venom, like poisonous snakes. It has short teeth, but they are all venomous, and the venom is strong enough to kill an adult human.

STINGRAY

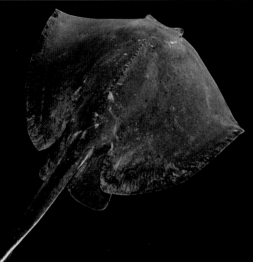

The Stingray is closely related to sharks, but you do not have to worry about its bite – it's the sting in the tail that's the problem. This fish likes shallow water, and often hides in the sand on the seabed. Unwary swimmers and paddlers are liable to be speared by the long, venomous spine that is located near the base of the Stingray's long tail.

HARVESTER ANT

Harvester ants are common in the United States of America. They like to collect plant seeds without any disturbance. If any human beings get in their way – maybe while having a picnic – then the humans had better watch out! Harvester ants are equipped with a sharp sting that injects dangerous venom. Pain and itching are immediate, and death sometimes follows.

WESTERN DIAMOND BACK RATTLESNAKE

The Western diamond-Back is the strongest and most aggressive of the North American rattlesnakes. This highly dangerous snake prefers to keep its venom for prey that is small enough for it to swallow. Large intruders are warned by the distinctive rattle, and they had better beware – this killer bites fast and bites deep.

NO. 10 POISON DART FROG

		Extreme Scores	
Animal type	Amphibian	**Shape**	3
Location	Central and South America	**Danger**	5
Size	2-6cm	**Attack**	5
Diet	Mainly insects	**Lethal**	7
Habitat	Rainforest		
Notable feature	Poisonous skin	**Prey**	3

TOTAL SCORE **23** / 50

NO. 9 SYDNEY FUNNEL-WEB SPIDER

		Extreme Scores	
Animal type	Arachnid	**Shape**	8
Location	Australia	**Danger**	4
Size	2-4cm	**Attack**	4
Diet	Insects, amphibians, etc.	**Lethal**	3
Habitat	Mostly woodland		
Notable feature	Deadly venom	**Prey**	5

TOTAL SCORE **24** / 50

NO. 8 BLUE-RINGED OCTOPUS

		Extreme Scores	
Animal type	Cephalopod	**Shape**	6
Location	Indo-Pacific	**Danger**	5
Size	10cm	**Attack**	6
Diet	Crabs and fish	**Lethal**	5
Habitat	Indian and Pacific Oceans		
Notable feature	Deadly saliva	**Prey**	6

TOTAL SCORE **28** / 50

NO. 7 STONEFISH

		Extreme Scores	
Animal type	Bony fish	**Shape**	5
Location	Indo-Pacific	**Danger**	7
Size	60cm	**Attack**	7
Diet	Shrimps and small fish	**Lethal**	5
Habitat	Indian and Pacific ocean		
Notable feature	Deadly spines	**Prey**	5

TOTAL SCORE **29** / 50

NO. 6 PALESTINE SCORPION

		Extreme Scores	
Animal type	Aracnid	**Shape**	7
Location	Middle East	**Danger**	8
Size	8-11cm	**Attack**	4
Diet	Insects	**Lethal**	9
Habitat	Deserts and scrubland		
Notable feature	Deadly sting	**Prey**	4

TOTAL SCORE **32** / 50

NO. 5 FIERCE SNAKE

Animal type	Reptile	Extreme Scores		TOTAL SCORE
Location	Australia	Shape		6
Size	2.5m	Danger		6
Diet	Small mammals	Attack	35/50	8
Habitat	Forests and plains	Lethal		9
Notable feature	Deadly venom	Prey		6

NO. 4 ANOPHELES MOSQUITO

Animal type	Insect	Extreme Scores		TOTAL SCORE
Location	Worldwide	Shape		2
Size	8mm	Danger		9
Diet	Mammal blood	Attack	36/50	6
Habitat	Around water	Lethal		10
Notable feature	Transmits disease	Prey		9

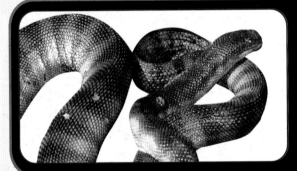

NO. 3 BEAKED SEA SNAKE

Animal type	Reptile	Extreme Scores		TOTAL SCORE
Location	Indo-Pacific	Shape		7
Size	2m	Danger		8
Diet	Fish, fish eggs and eels	Attack	37/50	8
Habitat	Pacific Ocean	Lethal		8
Notable feature	Deadly venom	Prey		6

NO. 2 PIRANHA

Animal type	Bony fish	Extreme Scores		TOTAL SCORE
Location	South America	Shape		4
Size	30-60cm	Danger		9
Diet	Fish, crabs and mammals	Attack	40/50	10
Habitat	Rivers	Lethal		7
Notable feature	Razor sharp teeth	Prey		10

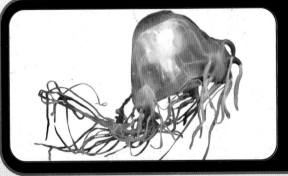

NO. 1 SEA WASP JELLYFISH

Animal type	Cnidarian	Extreme Scores		TOTAL SCORE
Location	Indo-Pacific	Shape		10
Size	30cm	Danger		10
Diet	Shrimp and small fish	Attack	41/50	6
Habitat	Sea around Australia	Lethal		8
Notable feature	Stinging tentacles	Prey		7

This section is a catalogue of the world's top ten predators. Predators are nature's born killers, it is what they do – they must kill in order to eat. There are many different animals that are predators, including mammals, birds, reptiles and fish. But which is the best? Our top ten predators were rated according to:

BODY MASS Size is obviously important for a predator. The bigger the predator, the bigger the prey it can attack. Similarly with weight, a heavy predator will find it easier to drag down and overpower its prey. We gave our predators a combined score based on their size and weight, but also taking into consideration the average size of their prey in each case.

NO.1 | GREAT WHITE SHARK

The great white shark is the world's deadliest and most dangerous predator. It is found near cool and temperate coastlines across the globe. Armed with jaws more than 60 centimetres wide, the great white shark has a superb sense of smell and can detect wounded prey several miles away.

BODY MASS
Measuring up to 8 metres in length, a great white shark can weigh more than 3,000 kilograms.

SPEED
It is a fast swimmer, especially when chasing prey, and can leap its entire body out of the water.

TEETH AND CLAWS
Rows of triangular teeth line the great white's massive jaws. Each tooth is serrated like a steak knife and is razor sharp.

KILLER INSTINCT
The great white attacks prey with a twisting lunge tearing a chunk of flesh from the victim. The shark then retreats and waits for the victim to die from loss of blood.

SPEED

High speed gives a predator a tremendous advantage. The cheetah, which is the world's fastest animal, was clearly the winner in this category. With the others, we also looked at whether the animals could leap, and how far. We also gave extra points to crocodiles because they can move on land as well as in water.

TEETH AND CLAWS

This category examines the tools of the predators' trade – the deadly weapons that are used to kill their prey. We based our score on the number, length and sharpness of the teeth and claws of each predator. These scores were adjusted according to whether it is the teeth or the claws that are the primary offensive weapons.

KILLER INSTINCT

Here we look at the overall style of each predator's attack. We gave points for hunting technique, stealth and camouflage. Additional points went to those predators that were able to achieve the all-important element of surprise, taking their prey unawares. We also gave bonus points to those animals that had highly developed senses for locating prey.

PREY

Few predators specialise in just one kind of prey. Most are generalists that will attack anything that they can kill and eat – especially if they have not eaten for some time and are very hungry. Points were allocated according to the size and variety of prey that is normally taken. Extra points went to those predators that sometimes feast on human flesh.

These teeth are designed to slice rather than grip. Each tooth lasts for less than a year before being replaced by a fresh tooth.

EXTREME SCORES

Our top predator – a **cold-blooded** killer that is the most efficient and ferocious hunter on earth.

BODY MASS
9/10

SPEED
4/10

TEETH AND CLAWS
10/10

KILLER INSTINCT
10/10

PREY
10/10

= TOTAL SCORE

PREY

The main prey animals are seals, dolphins, and large fish (including other sharks), but the great white will attack anything it thinks it can eat.

103

LEOPARD

The leopard is a secretive and deadly predator that only comes out to hunt at night. Powerful limb and neck muscles make it the strongest climber of the big cats. The leopard lives in warm and cool climates throughout Asia and Africa, and is found in both open country and dense forest.

BODY MASS

This agile hunter weighs about 65 kilograms. Most leopards have pale fur with black spots, but some are entirely black. These black leopards are known as panthers.

SPEED

Very few people have ever seen a leopard run at top speed, but it can reach about 60 kph and can leap across a gap 6 metres wide.

TEETH AND CLAWS

The leopard has broad paws with curved claws that end in very sharp points. Its canine teeth are longer proportionally than in any other big cat.

Spotted fur provides excellent camouflage when stalking prey.

KILLER INSTINCT

This big cat may sneak up on its prey through tall grass. Or it may wait in ambush on a tree branch, before jumping down to sink its teeth into its victim's neck.

PREY

Although it can attack and kill prey as big as a giraffe, the leopard mainly hunts smaller mammals such as **antelope**, deer and wild pigs.

Eyes positioned at the front of the head indicate that this animal is a predator.

This **nocturnal** predator is a deadly killer that combines stealth with powerful muscles and sharp claws.

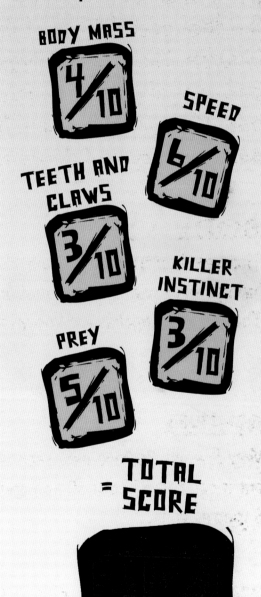

BODY MASS
4/10

SPEED
6/10

TEETH AND CLAWS
3/10

KILLER INSTINCT
3/10

PREY
5/10

= TOTAL SCORE

The coyote is a North American wild dog that has adapted to a wide variety of environments. It is found from the hot deserts of Mexico to the frozen forests of Alaska and northern Canada. The coyote is a highly efficient predator that hunts by both night and day.

BODY MASS

The coyote is about the size of a German Shepherd dog, but much slimmer. The average coyote weighs about 14 kg, and the male is slightly heavier than the female.

SPEED

Coyotes can run at speeds of up to 48 kph for short burst but can maintain a 32 kph lope for long periods.

TEETH AND CLAWS

Its claws are sharp, but teeth are the coyote's main weapons. There are 42 in all, including four long, pointed canine teeth.

A coyote uses its eyes, ears and nose to locate prey.

Parents fetch food for young coyote pups.

Snow, rock, grassland or desert – it's all the same to this **adaptable** predator.

KILLER INSTINCT

The coyote usually hunts alone, and can chase **prey** over long distances without getting tired. It has an excellent sense of smell for sniffing out prey hiding underground.

PREY

The coyote hunts a wide variety of prey; mainly small mammals, such as mice, rabbits and squirrels, but also birds, snakes, and lizards. It will also kill cats and dogs in urban areas.

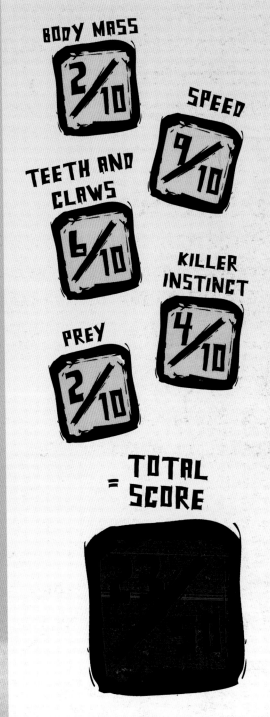

BODY MASS
2/10

SPEED
9/10

TEETH AND CLAWS
6/10

KILLER INSTINCT
4/10

PREY
2/10

= TOTAL SCORE

POLAR BEAR

The polar bear lives in the **Arctic** region surrounding the North Pole. It is the largest and most powerful predator that lives on land, and it has nothing to fear – except hunger. A polar bear needs to spend about half its waking life hunting, because it is only successful once or twice in every hundred attempts.

BODY MASS

A polar bear has a huge body covered in shaggy fur. It can weigh up to 700 kilograms and is more than 3 metres long.

TEETH AND CLAWS

It has long, sharp claws that can easily rip through skin and muscle. Its powerful jaws can crunch through bones.

PREY

The main food items are seals, but polar bears also **prey** on fish, seabirds, walruses and reindeer.

Pale fur provides camouflage against the snow-covered landscape.

Powerful muscles are the key to the polar bear's deadly attack.

Insulated from the cold by a thick fur coat, this Arctic killer is a powerful predator.

KILLER INSTINCT

The polar bear usually catches seals when they are out of the water or come to the surface to breathe. Sometimes a polar bear will break through ice to get at a seal underneath.

SPEED

A polar bear can run across snow and ice at speeds of up to 40 kph. It is also an excellent swimmer.

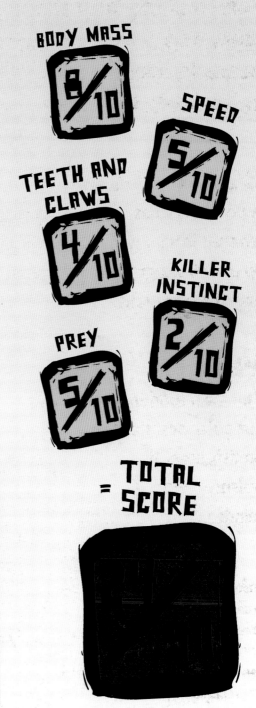

BODY MASS
8/10

SPEED
5/10

TEETH AND CLAWS
4/10

KILLER INSTINCT
2/10

PREY
5/10

= TOTAL SCORE

ROYAL BENGAL TIGER

The Royal Bengal tiger is one of the largest of the tiger sub-species, and it rivals the Siberian tiger for the title "Biggest of the Big Cats". The Royal Bengal tiger is found in parts of northern India and Pakistan. Like all tigers, it is a deadly predator, and it can develop a taste for human flesh.

BODY MASS

The Royal Bengal tiger is the second-largest tiger in the world. It weighs between 200-250 kilograms, and can measure 2.8 metres in length.

No two tigers have exactly the same pattern of stripes.

SPEED

This tiger is one of the fastest animals in the world. They can only sprint for a short distance, but these tigers can reach speeds of nearly 61 kph.

This predator leaps onto its prey with claws outstretched and jaws gaping wide.

TEETH AND CLAWS

The Royal Bengal tiger has strong, sharp claws and powerful jaws equipped with 30 sharp teeth. It has the biggest canine teeth of any animal in the world.

KILLER INSTINCT

Royal Bengal tigers leap onto their prey, digging in with their claws to drag their victim to the ground.

PREY

This tiger will attack animals larger than itself, and its main prey is deer. It can eat more than 40 kilograms of meat at a time.

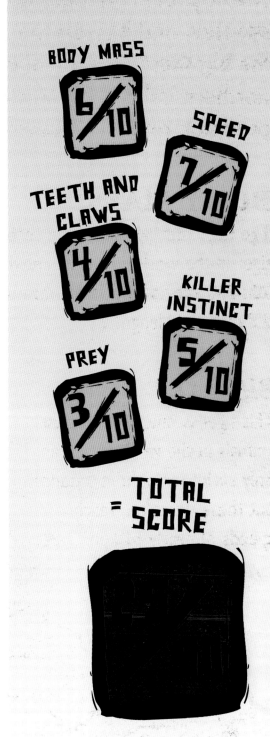

This tiger is the largest and most awesome of the big cats. It is a born predator.

BODY MASS
6/10

SPEED
7/10

TEETH AND CLAWS
4/10

KILLER INSTINCT
5/10

PREY
3/10

= TOTAL SCORE

CHEETAH

The cheetah is the fastest thing on four legs – it can run quicker than any other animal on Earth. The super-fast cheetah is one of the smallest of the big cats, but it is also one of the deadliest. The cheetah lives on the grasslands of Africa, where it uses its speed to catch fast-running prey.

BODY MASS

The cheetah has a slim, lightweight body, and weighs only about 40-45 kilograms.

The cheetah has a very distinctive body shape.

SPEED

Over short distances a cheetah can reach a speed of nearly 113 kph.

TEETH AND CLAWS

The cheetah attacks with both teeth and claws in a highly efficient "catch and cling" technique.

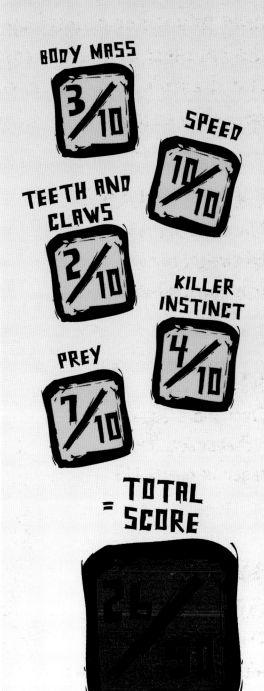

Sharp claws and teeth drag down
a helpless victim.

KILLER INSTINCT

A cheetah usually hunts at sunrise and
sunset. It will stealthily creep
through the grass until it is
close enough to its prey to
launch a high-speed attack.

PREY

The cheetah hunts
rabbits and small
mammals, as well as
larger prey such as
zebra and antelope.

No animal can run fast enough
to escape the high-speed attack
launched by this predator.

BODY MASS
3/10

SPEED
10/10

TEETH AND CLAWS
2/10

KILLER INSTINCT
4/10

PREY
7/10

= TOTAL SCORE
26/50

The great horned owl is a deadly predator that can kill prey up to three times its own size. It is so deadly that it has earned the nickname "the tiger of the woods". The great horned owl is found throughout North, Central and South America and lives in abandoned nests, trees or even caves.

BODY MASS

The great horned owl weighs about 2.5 kilograms and stands over half a metre tall with a wingspan of up to a metre and a half. Females are larger than males.

SPEED

This majestic bird has a maximum flying speed of nearly 61 kph. It attacks silently and without warning, swooping down from its perch to seize its prey on the ground.

TEETH AND CLAWS

The great horned owl has no teeth, but it does have a sharp **beak** for tearing flesh. Its main weapons are the sharp pointed **talons** on its feet.

Sharp eyes and keen hearing are the key to the owl's success as a hunter.

KILLER INSTINCT

The great horned owl is most active at night. They use their sense of sight and hearing to find prey. They are stealth hunters and dive down from high perches to snatch their prey.

PREY

A great horned owl is capable of taking prey much bigger than itself. Its diet includes skunks, foxes and even porcupines.

The coloration of the feathers provides excellent camouflage against tree trunks and branches.

This bird is a silent killer that swoops down out of the darkness without warning.

BODY MASS
1/10

SPEED
9/10

TEETH AND CLAWS
4/10

KILLER INSTINCT
7/10

PREY
6/10

= TOTAL SCORE
27/10

The Nile crocodile is found in rivers, lakes and swamps throughout most of Africa. It is a **cold-blooded** killer, but rather a lazy hunter. This large **reptile** prefers to lie in ambush, with only its eyes and nostrils showing above the river surface, waiting for prey to come near enough for it to strike.

BODY MASS

Nile crocodiles can grow up to 6 metres in length. They are covered in natural armour made of bony plates embedded in the skin.

A crocodile swims by using its flattened tail as a paddle.

TEETH AND CLAWS

The claws are fairly blunt and are mainly used for digging nests in the riverbank. Long jaws full of sharp teeth are the Nile crocodile's main weapons.

SPEED

The Nile crocodile swims at about 6-10 kph. On land it can run at almost twice that speed.

These long, sharp teeth can inflict terrible wounds.

KILLER INSTINCT

Like other reptiles, the Nile crocodile can bite, but it cannot chew. Small prey is swallowed whole. Larger prey is grabbed and dragged underwater to drown.

PREY

Small prey includes fish and water birds, but animals as big as buffalos and giraffe are attacked when they drink or wade across rivers.

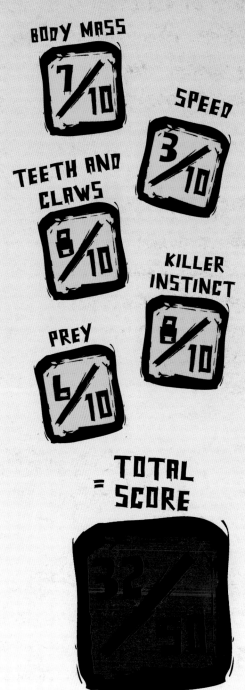

EXTREME SCORES

At first glance it might look like a log of wood floating in the water – but that "log" is actually one of the most feared of all predators.

BODY MASS
7/10

SPEED
3/10

TEETH AND CLAWS
8/10

KILLER INSTINCT
8/10

PREY
6/10

= TOTAL SCORE

Although it is famous as the "King of the Jungle", the African lion is rarely seen in a rain forest environment. This powerful predator prefers the open grasslands of the **savannah** or **veldt**. Unlike other big cats, which are usually solitary hunters, the African lion often hunts in small groups of between three and eight animals.

BODY MASS

African lions can reach lengths of over 3 metres, and can weigh up to 250 kilograms. The male is larger than the female lioness.

SPEED

The African lion is not a good or fast runner, but it can reach about 55 kph over very short distances.

TEETH AND CLAWS

These lions have five claws on each paw. Its powerful jaws are packed full with 30 sharp teeth that can lock together like a vice.

The lion is Africa's top predator.

Male lions are the only big cats
with a mane of long fur.

KILLER INSTINCT

Lions usually co-operate with each other when
hunting. Several members of a lion group will
try to drive the prey towards other lions.

PREY

The African lion hunts
mainly large mammals.
These **prey** include
zebra, gnus, impala
and wildebeest.

EXTREME SCORES

The technique of cooperative
hunting gives this big cat a deadly
advantage over all the others.

BODY MASS
6/10

SPEED
8/10

TEETH AND
CLAWS
5/10

KILLER
INSTINCT
7/10

PREY
8/10

= TOTAL
SCORE

34/50

ORCA (KILLER WHALE)

The orca, or killer whale, is a toothed whale that is closely related to dolphins and porpoises. This marine mammal is found in seas and oceans around the world, although it prefers cooler water and is rarely seen in the tropics. The orca deserves its popular name because it is a deadly, top predator with no natural enemies.

BODY MASS

A fully-grown orca normally measures around 7 metres but lengths of nearly 10 metres have been recorded! These whales can weigh up to 10,000 kilograms. Males are bigger than the females.

The orca has a distinctive black-and-white coloration.

SPEED

Orcas are fast swimmers. They can reach over 48 kph in short bursts when chasing their prey.

TEETH AND CLAWS

An orca has 40-46 large, pointed teeth, but it cannot chew and has to swallow its prey whole.

KILLER INSTINCT

Orcas often live and hunt in small family groups that are known as pods, and the members of a pod often co-operate while hunting. Individual orcas will even seize sea lions that are resting on a beach.

The smiling face of a born killer.

This is one of the biggest predators on Earth – about 10 tonnes of killing power.

BODY MASS
10/10

SPEED
5/10

TEETH AND CLAWS
9/10

KILLER INSTINCT
9/10

PREY
9/10

= **TOTAL SCORE**

PREY

Orca feed mainly on fish (especially salmon), but they also hunt dolphins, whales, squid, seals, sea lions, penguins, and marine turtles.

GREAT WHITE SHARK

The great white shark is the world's deadliest and most dangerous predator. It is found near cool and **temperate** coastlines across the globe. Armed with jaws more than 60 centimetres wide, the great white shark has a superb sense of smell and can detect wounded prey several kilometres away.

BODY MASS

Measuring up to 8 metres in length, a great white shark can weigh more than 3,000 kilograms.

SPEED

It is a fast swimmer, especially when chasing prey, and can leap its entire body out of the water.

TEETH AND CLAWS

Rows of triangular teeth line the great white's massive jaws. Each tooth is serrated like a steak-knife and is razor sharp.

KILLER INSTINCT

The great white attacks prey with a twisting lunge tearing a chunk of flesh from the victim. The shark then retreats and waits for the victim to die from loss of blood.

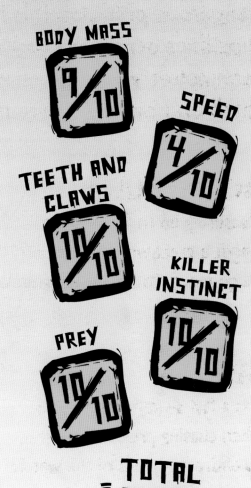

These teeth are designed to slice rather than grip. Each tooth lasts for less than a year before being replaced by a fresh tooth.

EXTREME SCORES

Our top predator – a **cold-blooded** killer that is the most efficient and ferocious hunter on Earth.

BODY MASS
9/10

SPEED
4/10

TEETH AND CLAWS
10/10

KILLER INSTINCT
10/10

PREY
10/10

= TOTAL SCORE

43/50

PREY

The main prey animals are seals, dolphins, and large fish (including other sharks), but the great white will attack anything it thinks it can eat.

CLOSE
BUT NOT CLOSE ENOUGH

Before deciding our Top Ten Predators, we also considered these animals – all of them are skilled and efficient hunters, but they are not quite good enough to make the Top Ten.

BALD EAGLE

The bald eagle is the national bird of the United States of America. It is not really bald, but the white feathers on its head and neck make it look bald from a distance. It is a large, powerful bird that weighs up to 6 kilograms and has a wingspan of up to 2.5 metres. The bald eagle is especially fond of fish, and swoops down to seize salmon in its sharp talons.

TARANTULA

Tarantulas are the largest of all spiders and they are widespread throughout tropical regions. The biggest tarantulas have a leg span of nearly 30 centimetres and can move very quickly. Tarantulas do not spin webs; they are active hunters that prowl around at night looking for **prey** such as mice and small birds.

VAMPIRE BAT

This small South American mammal has a fearsome reputation because of its diet – it feeds on the blood of other mammals. The vampire bat does not actually suck blood; it bites its victim to make the blood flow, then laps it up with its tongue. Although it can fly, this bat likes to walk and it is more likely to attack its prey from the ground.

WOLVERINE

The wolverine is the largest and fiercest member of the weasel family. It lives in the coniferous forests of Europe, Asia and North America. The wolverine measures up to 1.5 metres from nose to tail, and weighs about 15 kilograms. It chases after small prey such as hares and rabbits; and will climb trees so that it can jump down on large prey such as deer.

PANGOLIN

This strange scale-covered mammal is found in Africa and Asia. Although it is not at all fierce, the pangolin is in its own way a mighty hunter. It uses its powerful claws to burrow into termite mounds and ant nests, and then slurps up their tasty eggs with its long tongue. The unique coat of hard scales protects the pangolin against ant bites and stings.

NO. 10 LEOPARD

Scientific name	Panthera pardus	Extreme Scores	
Animal type	Mammal	Body mass	4
Location	Africa, Asia	Speed	6
Size	2m	Teeth & Claws	3
Habitat	Grasslands and forest	Killer instinct	3
Notable feature	Agility	Prey	5

TOTAL SCORE 21/50

NO. 9 COYOTE

Scientific name	Canis latrans	Extreme Scores	
Animal type	Mammal	Body mass	2
Location	North and Central America	Speed	9
Size	95cm	Teeth & Claws	6
Habitat	Deserts, mountains, praries	Killer instinct	4
Notable feature	Hardy, sense of smell	Prey	2

TOTAL SCORE 23/50

NO. 8 POLAR BEAR

Scientific name	Ursus maritimus	Extreme Scores	
Animal type	Mammal	Body mass	8
Location	Artic	Speed	5
Size	3.4m	Teeth & Claws	4
Habitat	Arctic region	Killer instinct	2
Notable feature	Bulk and power	Prey	5

TOTAL SCORE 24/50

NO. 7 ROYAL BENGAL TIGER

Scientific name	Panther tigris tigris	Extreme Scores	
Animal type	Mammal	Body mass	6
Location	Asia	Speed	7
Size	2.8m	Teeth & Claws	4
Habitat	Forests, jungles and swamps	Killer instinct	5
Notable feature	Large canine teeth	Prey	3

TOTAL SCORE 24/50

NO. 6 CHEETAH

Scientific name	Acinonyx jubatus	Extreme Scores	
Animal type	Mammal	Body mass	3
Location	Africa	Speed	10
Size	1.5m	Teeth & Claws	2
Habitat	Grasslands	Killer instinct	4
Notable feature	Speed	Prey	7

TOTAL SCORE 26/50

NO. 5 GREAT HORNED OWL

Scientific name	*Bubo virginianus*	Extreme Scores		TOTAL SCORE
Animal type	Bird	Body mass	1	27/50
Location	The Americas	Speed	9	
Size	60cm	Teeth & Claws	4	
Habitat	Forest, woodland, shrubland	Killer instinct	7	
Notable feature	Keen sight	Prey	6	

NO. 4 NILE CROCODILE

Scientific name	*Crocodylus niloticus*	Extreme Scores		TOTAL SCORE
Animal type	Reptile	Body mass	7	32/50
Location	Africa	Speed	3	
Size	6m	Teeth & Claws	8	
Habitat	Rivers, lakes, marshes	Killer instinct	8	
Notable feature	Powerful jaws	Prey	6	

NO. 3 AFRICAN LION

Scientific name	*Panthera leo*	Extreme Scores		TOTAL SCORE
Animal type	Mammal	Body mass	6	34/50
Location	Africa	Speed	8	
Size	2.5m	Teeth & Claws	5	
Habitat	Savannah	Killer instinct	7	
Notable feature	Strength	Prey	8	

NO. 2 ORCA (KILLER WHALE)

Scientific name	*Orcinus orca*	Extreme Scores		TOTAL SCORE
Animal type	Mammal	Body mass	10	42/50
Location	Worldwide	Speed	5	
Size	7m	Teeth & Claws	9	
Habitat	Seas and oceans	Killer instinct	9	
Notable feature	Size and speed	Prey	9	

NO. 1 GREAT WHITE SHARK

Scientific name	*Carcharodon carcharias*	Extreme Scores		TOTAL SCORE
Animal type	Cartilaginous fish	Body mass	9	43/50
Location	Worldwide	Speed	4	
Size	8m	Teeth & Claws	10	
Habitat	Coastal and offshore waters	Killer instinct	10	
Notable feature	Killer instinct	Prey	10	

ADAPTABLE capable of adapting to a particular situation or use

AGILE something that can move quickly and easily

AMPHIBIAN an animal capable of living both on land and in water

ANTELOPE group of fast-running, grass-eating mammals native to Africa and Asia, with long horns and a slender build

ANTIDOTE a remedy used to neutralise the effects of a poison or venom

ARCTIC regions around the North Pole

BEAK a bird's jaws

BIPEDAL a two-footed animal

CAMOUFLAGE means of disguise by protective colouring or shape

CARCASS the dead body of an animal

CARNIVORE a meat-eating animal

CARRION the dead and rotting body of an animal

COLD-BLOODED an animal whose body temperature is not internally regulated

CORAL REEF a reef consisting of coral – the external skeleton of a group of marine animals

CREST a tuft or ridge on the head of a bird or other animal

CRETACEOUS the last period before the extinction of the dinosaurs – 146 to 65 million years ago

DESERT waterless area of land with little or no vegetation

DINOSAUR land-living reptiles that lived during the Triassic, Jurassic and Cretaceous periods

EOCENE an epoch of history from 58 million to 40 million years ago when the first modern mammals appeared

EPOCH a unit or period of geologic time

FANG a hollow tooth of a venomous snake with which it injects its poison, or a canine tooth of a carnivorous animal with which it seizes and tears its prey

FOSSIL the remains of a dead animal that has turned to stone

GLAND organ of the body which secretes chemical substances

HADROSAUR group of large bipedal dinosaurs that had a horny, duck-like bill and webbed feet

HEART organ that pumps blood through the circulatory system

HERBIVORE a plant-eating animal

ICE AGE any period of time during which glaciers covered a large part of the Earth's surface. The most recent occurred from 2 million to 11 thousand years ago

JAWS the structures that form the framework of the mouth and hold the teeth

JOINT a point of the body that enables two bones to move

JURASSIC the middle period when dinosaurs were a dominant species on Earth – 208 to 146 million years ago

LATIN an ancient language still used by scientists to give the official name of animal species

MALARIA infectious disease characterised by cycles of chills, fever, and sweating transmitted to humans by the bite of an infected female Anopheles mosquito

MAMMAL any of various warm-blooded animals with a covering of hair on the skin and, in the female, the ability to produce milk with which to feed the young

MARINE something of, relating to, or produced by the sea

MICROBE a minute life form; a micro-organism, especially a bacterium that causes disease

MIOCENE an epoch of time from 25 million to 13 million years ago, that saw the appearance of grazing mammals

NOCTURNAL a creature that is active during the night

NOSTRILS either of the external openings of the nose

OLIGOCENE an epoch of time from 40 million to 25 million years ago, that saw the appearance of sabre-toothed cats

OMNIVORE an animal that eats both meat and plants

OSTRICH large, swift-running flightless bird of Africa. It has a long bare neck, small head, and two-toed feet. It is the largest living bird

PALAEONTOLOGIST scientist who specialises in the study of fossil organisms and related remains

PINCERS front claw of a lobster, crab, or similar creature

PLIOCENE the last epoch of the Tertiary period that saw the appearance of modern looking animals

PREDATOR an animal that lives by preying on other animals

PREY an animal hunted or caught for food

RAIN FOREST a dense evergreen forest occupying a tropical region with an annual rainfall of at least 2.5 metres

REPTILE a cold-blooded animal that has scales and lays eggs on land

SALIVA watery liquid secreted into the mouth by glands

SAVANNAH flat grassland of tropical or subtropical regions

SERRATED notched like the edge of a saw

SHOAL a large group of fish or other marine animals

SPECIES a class of individuals or objects grouped by virtue of their common attributes and assigned a common name

SPINE series of vertebrae forming the axis of the skeleton and protecting the spinal cord

STAMINA lasting strength and energy

STING a sharp, piercing organ or part, often ejecting a venomous secretion

SUB-SPECIES subdivision (a race or variety) of a species

TALON the claw of a bird of prey or predatory animal

TEMPERATE a region free from extremes of temperature

TENTACLE a flexible organ near the head or mouth in many animals used for feeling or grasping

TERTIARY period of time from 63 million to 2 million years ago, that saw the appearance of modern flora, apes and other large mammals

THEROPOD group of carnivorous dinosaurs with short forelimbs that walked or ran on strong hind legs

TOXIN a poisonous substance that is produced by living cells or organisms capable of causing disease when introduced into the body

TROPICAL hot and humid; relating to the tropics, a region on either side of the Equator

TUSK a long pointed tooth specialised for fighting or digging; especially in an elephant or walrus

VELDT open grazing areas of southern Africa

VENOM a poisonous secretion of an animal, such as a snake, spider, or scorpion, usually transmitted by a bite or sting

VENOMOUS a creature that can produce venom

INDEX